INSPIRED
TO SOAR!

ALSO BY T.D. JAKES

INSPIRED TO SOAR!

101 Daily Readings for
Building Your Vision

T.D. JAKES

New York   Nashville

FaithWords
Hachette Book Group
1290 Avenue of the Americas, New York, NY 10104
faithwords.com
twitter.com/faithwords

First Edition: August 2018

FaithWords is a division of Hachette Book Group, Inc. The FaithWords name and logo are trademarks of Hachette Book Group, Inc.

The publisher is not responsible for websites (or their content) that are not owned by the publisher.

The Hachette Speakers Bureau provides a wide range of authors for speaking events. To find out more, go to www.hachettespeakersbureau.com or call (866) 376-6591.

Library of Congress Cataloging-in-Publication Data has been applied for.

ISBNs: 978-1-5460-1038-8 (paper over board), 978-1-5460-1043-2 (ebook)

Printed in the United States of America

LSC-C

10 9 8 7 6 5 4 3 2 1

Contents

Introduction

I've written *Soar! Build Your Vision from the Ground Up* with the young entrepreneur as well as the successful business leader in mind. I want to help you create a business that will take flight and then soar. I also want to share with you from my experiences as an entrepreneur ways to keep growing and sustaining your flight.

I use the analogy of flying because launching and running a successful business is a lot like taking off and flying. In order to fly—and start a business—you need to overcome the inherent fear of leaving the safety of solid ground to defy gravity, navigate through unexpected variables within predictable patterns, and soar.

In this book, I use the stories and information from my book *Soar* in bite-sized pieces, prepared in daily readings to help you digest the information regularly. I've included scriptures to match the themes of the readings to give you a Biblical perspective, which can further undergird you and prepare you for what is ahead.

You will see that the Wright Brothers, the inventors of the first airplane to actually take flight, are one of my favorite examples of successful entrepreneurs. What they did back in the early 1900s changed our lives forever. Their model of innovative, relentless tenacity is one we can all glean inspiration from. These brothers made the seemingly impossible become a new reality.

And I believe that's exactly what every entrepreneur does. So with your ideas in mind, don't give up on creating what may seem impossible. As you work through this book, I will offer my thoughts and suggestions on this journey. I hope to help you catch the vision, build your wings, check the weather conditions, launch, and soar to new heights.

You've been cleared for take off…so let's go!

Take Off

He fills my life with good things. My youth is renewed like the eagle's!

(Psalm 103:5, NLT)

Do you remember your first time flying in a plane or even seeing one take off? If you had a similar experience as I did, you were captivated by the huge plane that was able to lift off of the ground and enter the air. Once the wheels of the plane were tucked in, you felt the plane pick up speed and sustain itself in the friendly skies. It was and still is amazing.

You, thousands of feet in the air, are able to see the beautiful, puffy clouds just outside your window. What were once far away are now so close you may think you can reach out and touch them.

Flying for the first time is a lot like creating your own business, launching a start-up, or establishing a nonprofit organization. In order to lift off, you have to overcome the inherent fear of leaving the safety of the solid ground behind. The journey to entrepreneurship is filled with unexpected variables and it requires just a bit of crazy and a lot of courage.

The Wright brothers are a great example of what it takes to get a business off the ground. Orville and Wilbur used scrap materials from a bicycle shop to build wings that would change the transportation world forever. Their curiosity and vision drove them to try and fail and try some more. They passionately pursued innovation and eventually transformed inspiration and perspiration into aviation.

You too, my friend, can take off like an airplane or even an eagle and soar into the sky. If you are willing to put in the work, follow your heart, and take a risk, your dreams of owning a business can take flight.

Are you ready to take off?

Look Inside

Instead, let the Spirit renew your thoughts and attitudes.   (Ephesians 4:23, NLT)

As you prepare to launch your business venture—or take your business to another level—I encourage you to take a look inside of yourself. You can't fly high without checking your internal gauges and ensuring they are ready for your flight.

I believe the ascendancy on the outside begins with the transcendence of a personal vision for what you can be. This starts on the inside so look at yourself. What do you see? What do you want to create to solve a problem or issue? What do you think people need? Why do you want to launch out on your own?

Your dreams begin internally and serve as the fuel to bring them into reality. Don't let go of the reason you have decided to take a leap and do something different and new. You will need this internal desire to keep you moving when things get cloudy and difficult. What drives you today can keep you moving forward when everything else says to stop.

Spend time trying to capture in words how you feel and why you are launching. You may need to refer back to your thoughts in the middle of this journey. Don't underestimate the power of your own words to motivate you.

And don't forget the power of God's Spirit can renew you and provide you with energy and insight. Keep your thoughts and attitudes focused as you prepare to take off.

Why did you start your business—or why do you want to launch?

We can rejoice, too, when we run into problems and trials, for we know that they help us develop endurance. And endurance develops strength of character, and character strengthens our confident hope of salvation.   (Romans 5:3-4, NLT)

What needs fixing, changing, or solving? This is a great question to ask yourself as you look to build a business. It's a great idea to offer a solution to a problem. Lots of people want solutions—and your providing an answer can not only help others but yield profits for you and your business.

Look outside in and isolate a problem or condition that may currently be affecting the social and cultural climate around you. Is there a need for a new product or invention that can help people with a certain lifestyle due to changes in technology, the economy, or perhaps migration patterns? Have environmental or political changes caused problems for those around you? Find a solution to assist them and you have found a viable business idea.

To turn your idea into a business or to expand your current business assess the time, talents and treasure that have been placed in your life. Use them to the fullest to employ strategies that can solve problems and provide a need for your community.

We often get frustrated from problems—in our personal lives or in our business. But changing your thoughts to focus on the solutions rather than just the problems can inspire innovation that can transcend into a successful business. It's all in how you see it.

What problems do you want to solve?

Here on earth you will have many trials and sorrows; but cheer up, for I have overcome the world. (John 16:33, TLB)

As we continue to look at how you view problems, I think it helps to take note of what is happening in your life. Are you exhausted from dead-end positions, pointless relationships, and indifferent environments? Often times because of these circumstances, you are forced to make a change. And that change can bring about good.

Successful entrepreneurs have learned not to curse the dark but to look for opportunities to share the light. Do not allow times and circumstances to derail you. Use them to push you to greater heights of innovation and invention.

You can use the blunders from your past to set a new course if you view them more as stepping stones than as failures. Bad models you've observed can push you to create change and do something differently. Use the wisdom garnered from what you've experienced and observed along with your talent and drive to arrive at a new destination. It can happen, depending on how you view the trials and sorrows you inevitably encountered in life.

What trials have pushed you toward entrepreneurship?

> Then Caleb quieted the people before Moses, and said, "Let us go up at once and take possession of it; for we will certainly conquer it." But the men who had gone up with him said, "We are not able to go up against the people [of Canaan], for they are too strong for us."
>
> (Numbers 13:30-31, AMP)

If you are serious about pursing your dream as an entrepreneur, you no doubt can see 101 reasons why you shouldn't move forward. You may feel like the scouts, or spies, from the Israelites sent to check out the land God had promised His people in today's verses. The land was filled with milk and honey, which meant it was fruitful and prosperous and filled with great treasures. However, people who looked like giants to the scouts also occupied the land. In fact, compared to the people in that land of Canaan, the Israelites looked like grasshoppers (Numbers 13:33).

When you stare at the obstacles between your reality and your dream, you too may feel like a helpless grasshopper; your bank account may seem miniature compared to the expenses you will incur. Your staff may seem invisible compared to the amount of work greeting you in the face. Your courage can be like a speck compared to the job at hand.

But there is hope. If you have the faith of Caleb (and Joshua) you will not only see the beauty in the land, but you will remember the promise in that land. If God has told you to go, then get moving. Stand tall and take one step at a time. Declare that you are well able to conquer whatever stands in your way.

Do not be discouraged about the size or number of obstacles in your path. I'm a witness; God can do things you could not even imagine. Use the gifts that God has put inside of you, rely on God's strength, and activate your creativity to soar above any obstacles you encounter.

Instead of staring at the "giants" in front of you, rely on God and the giant ways He is able to accomplish what seems impossible.

What do you see: giants or God's promised help?

Now faith is confidence in what we hope for and assurance about what we do
not see.   (Hebrews 11:1, NIV)

When you decide to launch a business or expand it, there's one thing you'll surely need. It is faith. You can do all of your homework—and I urge you to; you can write an excellent business plan, study the conditions, employ the best help, test your market and product, but you can still be fearful. Taking the next step is often scary.

I encourage business developers to feel the fear and move forward any way. If you've done your homework, you are ready. Pick up some faith and move on.

When you have faith, you decide to believe in God's plans for your business as well as in yourself. You realize that everything you'd like is not always right in front of your face. You have to trust and believe that things will come or work themselves out eventually. Wise entrepreneurs know they do not have all of the answers and resources, but they make the decision to build their faith and go for it.

Oftentimes there's no safety net. Going after your dream requires that you take a leap—and jump into it. Working with risk is a part of building a successful business. You will need faith to take a risk in the beginning—and even more faith to keep soaring.

Learn to get comfortable with risks. They go hand-in-hand with success. Get comfortable with risk and growth's relationship, for the biggest risks can yield the best results.

Build your faith!

What's in Your Hand?

Then the Lord asked him, "What is that in your hand?"

"A shepherd's staff," Moses replied. "Throw it down on the ground," the Lord told him. So Moses threw down the staff, and it turned into a snake! Moses jumped back.

(Exodus 4:2-3, NLT)

Oftentimes when we set out to pursue our dreams, we want to start off at the top. We want to be an overnight success, producing excellent services and goods that impact the world. And that's not a bad goal—always shoot for the stars.

However, young entrepreneurs—those who are just starting their business ventures—need to be reminded to begin where they are. If we are not careful, we can become paralyzed because we do not have everything at our disposable to make our dreams come true. We can wonder if we have enough money, enough expertise, enough influence, etc.

New business owners can sound a lot like Moses in Exodus 4. If you read the beginning of the chapter, you'll see that Moses was filled with doubt when he was given his assignment from God to deliver the Israelites from the taskmaster Pharaoh. Moses wondered if anyone would believe that he was sent by God. Moses wondered if he had what it took to be successful.

But God had an answer to all of Moses's questions. God simply asked Moses what was in his hand. Moses, I'm sure looking at his hand and seeing only a staff used to guide sheep, answered God.

Then, God showed Moses what He could do with a simple shepherd's staff. God turned the staff into a snake.

I think God was telling Moses to start where he was; to use what he had to begin his venture.

And that's what budding business owners need to do, too. You won't have everything at the starting point, but take assessment of what you do have and use it to get started. Your skill with faith in God can produce much more than your excuses.

What's in your hand?

Use What You've Got

One day the widow of a member of the group of prophets came to Elisha and cried out, "My husband who served you is dead, and you know how he feared the Lord. But now a creditor has come, threatening to take my two sons as slaves."

"What can I do to help you?" Elisha asked. "Tell me, what do you have in the house?"

"Nothing at all, except a flask of olive oil," she replied.   (2 Kings 4:1-2, NLT)

In *Soar!* I tell the story of Robbie Montgomery, whom many of you may know as the owner of Sweetie Pies. Miss Robbie has restaurants in St. Louis and Beverly Hills and she also starred in her own reality show. People rave about the down home cooking you can get from Miss Robbie's establishment, but here's an even better story behind her success. Miss Robbie had a successful career as a singer—she was a backup vocalist for Ike and Tina Turner and worked with Dr. John, Joe Cocker, Stevie Wonder, and Barbra Streisand.

But her music career ended because of a lung condition. But as you can see, that didn't stop Miss Robbie. Yes, she had to give up her dream career in music but she didn't give up on herself. She searched for another career and her love of food led her to the restaurant business—and that's how we have Sweetie Pies.

Life can be rough and tough. Dreams can be deferred and shattered, but true leaders dig deep and persevere. It's just like the story of Elisha and the widow. This woman was at the very end of her rope, left with her dead husband's debt and two sons to care for. She didn't know what to do, but thankfully, she turned to the prophet Elisha. He asked her what she had in her house. She said she only had oil—and that's where her sweet spot was. Elisha told her to get some jars and keep filling them with oil, her product, her brand, all that she had. She obeyed and she had a profitable business—so profitable that she was able to pay off her debt and care for her sons (2 Kings 4:7).

What you need to start your business may be right in front of your eyes. It may seem like a simple talent to you, but when you mix it with faith and perseverance, it can become a blessing to you and others.

What's in your house?

But don't begin until you count the cost. For who would begin construction of a building without first calculating the cost to see if there is enough money to finish it?

(Matthew 14:28, NLT)

Most entrepreneurs I know are big dreamers. After all, it takes vision to make things happen. You have to "see" a goal before you realize it. But there is a time and place for everything. And sometimes it helps to start small and employ a measured approach to our dreams.

When our dreams exceed our resources and our vision transcends our present opportunities, it is okay to start small—or even re-strategize. I don't think it's a lack of faith; I think it is similar to what Jesus taught in today's verse. You have to count your cost, think about what you need to get to where you want to be, and observe your current situation as well. The example Jesus used was of a man building a house. Before he starts building, he has to see if he has enough money to complete the project. He doesn't wait until he's laid the foundation to see if he has enough money for the roof. No, the builder estimates how much he'll need before he gets started.

When thinking about starting your business or taking the next steps, be practical and consider how much money you will need to invest in your dream. Also, think about how much time you have available to you. Do you still need to work a full-time job while starting your business? Do you have the responsibility of caring for children or elders?

Modify your strategy to fit your reality. And keep going. Don't let your circumstances make you stop dreaming or moving forward—just do it with wisdom, knowing what you are dealing with.

Have you counted your costs?

Hear, my son, your father's instruction, and forsake not your mother's teaching,
for they are a graceful garland for your head and pendants for your neck…

(Proverbs 1:8-9, ESV)

When you are preparing to launch a business, it is important to know the conditions around you. And there's more than one way to study these conditions and make needed adjustments for your venture.

When I was starting my daytime television show, I turned to my friend Oprah for clues on what the conditions looked like. Given her past success in the arena, I thought she was the best forecaster I could utilize. As my friend, she encouraged me, but as a professional who had navigated through these waters for decades, she also cautioned me about the stormy weather associated with the business.

Oprah reminded me that the winds had changed since she started in the business. We talked about how when she first launched her show, only three major networks controlled the majority of programming. Cable channels and independent programming were nowhere near at the level they are now. And of course, the Internet and online viewing was not even a part of the equation. Now as a result of changing technology, most traditional television channels have lost almost 40 percent of their views. People are using Netflix, Hulu, and Amazon more and more. All of these conditions impacted how I would think about my program and how we would launch.

I knew before I even started the challenges I was facing because I had studied the conditions. The conditions didn't deter me, but they did give me valuable information and helped me gauge my risks. The conditions also impacted other decisions. I hired people who had been in the business for a while and had proven to be the best. I deliberately sought out people who could help us navigate the turbulence we would be facing.

While I decided to end the program after one season, I learned a lot about using the conditions to plan a venture. Information should be used just like the weather forecast—helping you decide what plans to alter.

Are you looking at the weather conditions for your business?

The town women said to Naomi, "Blessed be God! He didn't leave you without family to carry on your life. May this baby grow up to be famous in Israel! He'll make you young again! He'll take care of you in old age. And this daughter-in-law who has brought him into the world and loves you so much, why, she's worth more to you than seven sons!"   (Ruth 4:14-15, MSG)

No matter what season of life you are in—your dreams can become realities. People of all ages and backgrounds long for a challenge, and reaching for our goals is what keeps us alive and in tune with what God has placed inside of us.

Did you know that Black women spanning in ages and stages in life are the fastest-growing group of entrepreneurs in our country? Women of every age are finding their place and entering into the world of entrepreneurship in our global community.

Many are like Naomi from the book of Ruth; if you are not familiar with her story, consider reading the four short chapters in the book. It's a wonderful story of an older woman who has lost her husband and two sons. She returns to her hometown broken and empty, but she is fortunate enough (although she doesn't always realize it) to have her daughter-in-law, Ruth, accompany her. After a rough patch in her life, things turn around for Naomi. Her daughter-in-law remarries and has a child. Naomi gets to be a vital part of the child's village and care for him. Her hope is renewed. Her joy is restored. She can continue in life on a new chapter—thanks to her daughter-in-law's devotion and Naomi's wisdom.

At times our lives can look bleak and empty, even closed for business. But, if we keep the hope, we too can have a second, third, fourth chance to create something beautiful. Look forward to your new season.

For what are you hoping?

But Jesus beheld them, and said unto them, With men this is impossible; but with God all things are possible. (Matthew 19:26, KJV)

Successful entrepreneurs share one belief system in common. They all believe that the impossible can become a reality. And if you're going to make it, you too need to adopt this attitude.

The beauty of creating a business is believing in it—especially when you cannot yet see it manifesting. Believing that it can and will happen is what keeps you going; it's what will get you up before dawn and keep you up late at night.

If you're going to make it in this world of business, you're going to need to act like the Wright brothers. They believed they could fly; they believed they could get into the sky—and they didn't stop trying until their goal was met.

The Wright brothers had innovative, relentless tenacity to fuel their dreams. They used the power of one transformative belief that they held in place regardless of their circumstances. They believed and they achieved.

Christians know that there are some things humans just can't do; however, those humans who believe in God know that what humans can't do, God can. The Bible is filled with miracles performed by God and his son, Jesus; most were fueled by faith—people's belief.

What do you believe? It may seem impossible, but with trust in God and relentless tenacity, it can be possible. Go for it.

Believe it . . . achieve it.

Like an Eagle

But those who hope in the Lord will renew their strength. They will soar on wings like eagles; they will run and not grow weary, they will walk and not be faint.

(Isaiah 40:31, NIV)

In *Soar!,* I tell the story of the time I received inspiration from looking out of my bedroom window. No, I wasn't daydreaming. I was observing a pair of mourning doves nesting in a tree. This pair had three eggs that soon hatched and produced three little balls of fuzz. In a few days, these little fuzz balls began looking more like birds. In a few more days, I noticed that the biggest chick was perched on the edge of a branch. In another day, this chick had mustered up the nerve to fly away from the nest. It took some time. The chick started off stretching his wings, then hopping around a bit, then hopping to a nearby branch. And then he took the leap and flew to a higher branch. From there, this chick watched one of the other chicks begin the process—stretching his wings, then hopping around, and eventually flying.

Within a few days, I witnessed every bird fly away from the nest. I observed the power of patience, perseverance, and practice—all from my bedroom window. I was so inspired by this process I revisited a film project I had put on hold indefinitely. With the birds in mind, I read the script and tried to envision the movie. But in the midst of my thinking, a new idea emerged. Instead of making this story into a feature film, what about using it as a pilot for a limited-run series on one of the many providers of online entertainment such as Hulu, Netflix, or Amazon?

While I'm still waiting to see if the project flies, I revel at what I learned from the little chicks. They weren't born able to fly, but they were born with the potential to fly. They had to put into practice what they were born to do before it could become. They didn't give up when things got scary; instead they practiced and took it one step at a time.

Waiting on God to renew our strength and make new revelations can give us the wings we need to fly. We may not enter the world knowing how to do it, but we have what it takes inside of us. Like the chicks, we need to practice, believe, and take it one step at a time.

Do you believe you can fly?

Propelled from Inside

The wind blows wherever it pleases. You hear its sound, but you cannot tell where it comes from or where it is going. So it is with everyone born of the Spirit.

(John 3:8, NIV)

Entrepreneurs can find inspiration just about anywhere. Nature can especially reveal certain ideas to us. Consider the wind. No one can see it, but we know it is there, blowing, shifting tree branches from side to side. When the wind is particularly strong, we have to take precautions against being knocked down or having other items fall on us, or our property. The wind is powerful, yet as today's verse reminds us, you can't tell where the wind is coming from or where it is going.

And sometimes being an entrepreneur is much like the wind. People may not be able to see exactly where you are going, but they should be able to see your impact and effect. You see, just like the wind, entrepreneurs' vision is powerful. What may not be visible on the outside needs to begin on the inside. In fact, your personal vision is what begins any motion or movement.

While it may not be conveyed easily or adequately in language, your vision should propel you to make changes. It should propel you to take action and pursue your goals.

Make sure what's churning inside of you fuels your actions and steps. Don't worry about external appearances; you've got to move to the beat of your internal barometer. No one may know which way it is blowing but you.

How does the wind inspire you?

Make It Soar

And the Lord answered me: "Write the vision; make it plain on tablets, so he may run who reads it."

(Habbukuk 2:2, ESV)

I n *Soar!*, I write about both my parents and their entrepreneurial ventures. I was fortunate to have a first-hand look at their hard work and visions. I was able to learn what to do and what not to do in business.

My father was a hard worker who hustled. He was determined to take care of his family at any cost. From selling fish out of his old Ford truck to starting his own janitorial services with a mop and broom—and watching it grow to include more than fifty employees.

However, when my father's business reached a certain level, he didn't transition with it. He got his vision off the ground and built a successful business, but he never let go of the attitude that he had to do it all. He struggled with managing his business and employees. His vision was limited.

I think if he had been able to write—or articulate—his vision to others he trained and trusted, he wouldn't have felt he had to do it all.

Writing, whether on paper or in actions, your vision is important. It communicates plans so that others can pick it up and run with it. You don't need to be present all the time and at every meeting if you have articulated your vision; someone else will know what to do, how to do it and why do it. You can be off thinking of the next level, the next goal—or even rejuvenating your spirit for the next task at hand.

Think about who knows your vision. How clearly have you presented it to them? Who can you trust to share your vision and help you take your business to the next level?

Write your vision—and share it with someone you trust.

She considers a field and buys it; with the fruit of her hands she plants a vineyard.

(Proverbs 31:16, ESV)

As I've said, I had the benefit of observing both my parents' entrepreneurial endeavors. And I learned a lot from seeing their hard work. My mother was a teacher by day, but like most entrepreneurs, she didn't just stop with her day job. In fact, she used the little money she was able to save from that job and invested it in real estate. Until the day my mom died, she rented out small homes and apartments and collected fees on each of them.

My mom knew she had a family to help raise and limited time to pursue outside investments, but she didn't let her circumstances stop her. Instead, she found something that would fit within her schedule and still yield benefits.

I also remember her selling Avon, raising vegetables, and having me peddle them door-to-door. She basically did anything she could to help my dad support our family.

She embodied the description of the Proverbs 31 woman. Her job description was endless—and her family was blessed by her endeavors. In fact, her family rises up and calls her blessed (v. 28).

While Proverbs 31 points to a woman, I believe the description is true for entrepreneurs also. In order to take care of ourselves and our families, we will do many things. In order to have a business flourish, we will work several "odd" jobs to finance our true passion. Entrepreneurs do what they have to do to make their vision come to light. Whatever is needed, whatever has to be done, we get it done.

What do you need to do to get it done?

Be Patient

But the Holy Spirit produces this kind of fruit in our lives: love, joy, peace, patience, kindness, goodness, faithfulness…   (Galatians 5:22, NLT)

One of the dangers of pursuing your dream is expecting success to happen overnight. We live in a quick fix, microwave society. Millennials have grown up with social media in their hands; they see the fruit of success in tweets, Instagram pictures, and more. It can appear as if success happens with one click. But it doesn't.

Wise entrepreneurs know that ramp-up time is required and that delayed doesn't mean denied. A successful business takes time and patience to build. You need long-term strategies to sustain you; you need to make profits and not use them up immediately. You need to learn to pace yourself when it comes to spending and working and planning.

I think it helps to expect to have to wait, to expect delayed gratification, when building. Our expectations are paramount and can help us find the patience needed to run the marathon, not just a sprint.

Patience is a result of the fruit of the spirit. When we stay close to God and seek His guidance, we can yield what is needed to run this race. Graduation relies on what's gradual. Allow the spirit to produce in you the sweet scent of patience so you can stick it out and enjoy the process.

Pray for patience.

> For there is a proper time and procedure for every matter...
>
> (Ecclesiastes 8:6, NIV)

Timing is essential when trying to get your business off the ground and into flight. It's important to know the time—what has happened, what is happening, and what could possibly happen based off of these trends.

In *Soar!*, I tell about a venture I did with Bible and book publisher Thomas Nelson in the '90s and early 2000s. On the heels of the success of my book *Woman, Thou Art Loosed!* We wanted to offer additional products for the target audience looking to enhance their relationship with God. We produced a Bible with notes, commentary, and questions—much of it based on the themes in the book. We went a step further and packaged the book in the shape of a woman's purse to make it unique, stylish, portable, and easy to carry. The response was tremendous and many people shared that they were blessed by the product.

Now think about how this might work, or not work, in today's society, in the time we currently live. Many people have transitioned from carrying Bibles in those neat little carrying cases to carrying their Bibles on their smart phones or other portable devices through apps. There are some really neat versions of the Bible on apps and many people find them easier to use and definitely more convenient to carry. And many women love designer purses, which have increased in popularity and have even more unique designs. So our packaging may not be able to compete with the designs today.

Timing impacts how your product performs in the market. A wise entrepreneur will consider all of the conditions before launching forward.

How do the times impact your product or business?

Don't Give Up

Let us not become weary in doing good, for at the proper time we will reap a harvest if we do not give up.

(Galatians 6:9, NIV)

Whatever season you may find yourself in, it is important to not give up on your dreams. I know things can get hard and your dream can seem further away, but the story of the mythical Daedalus—as well as many verses in the Bible—reminds us to not grow weary when we encounter obstacles to obtaining our goals.

Daedalus was a skilled craftsman—as most entrepreneurs are. He had a gift and he was hired to use that gift to build a labyrinth for King Minos. The labyrinth was a prison designed by Daedalus for the king's enemies. Now when the king and Daedalus' relationship soured, the king used Daedalus's own design to imprison him. Can you imagine the frustration Daedalus must have felt? He knew he had designed the complicated maze with no way to escape—and there he was, trapped by his own skill. But Daedalus didn't let his frustration make him give up hope or become so weary that he stopped thinking. Daedalus came up with a plan. He created wings from branches and beeswax and found a way to exit the labyrinth vertically. He didn't give up. While the maze probably made him feel like he was going around in circles with no end, he used his creativity to come up with another solution.

We can learn a lot from Daedalus. For many of us, life has us going around in circles, finding obstacles at each bend in the road. And while we must do what we have to do in each season of life, our attitude can change our outlook. Whatever you feel like you're stuck doing, don't let that be your end. Resign to keep looking and hoping for a way out—even if it is unconventional way. Pursue your dream; follow the path that will allow you to do what's calling you. Don't grow weary. Your hard work and pursuit will pay off—if you don't give up.

Create a sign or Post-it note to remind you to never give up hope.

That's why we can be so sure that every detail in our lives of love for God is worked into something good.   (Romans 8:28, MSG)

And we know that for those who love God all things work together for good, for those who are called according to his purpose.   (Romans 8:28, ESV)

Taking a look back over your life can sometimes give you the push you need to keep moving forward. Think about it: What has gotten you to the point where you are today? You may not be where you want to be; you may feel as if you're far off. But, taking inventory of your past can help you gain perspective on where you really are and all you've come through.

Even your negative experiences have shaped you and propelled you to a new place. Think about those seemingly dead-end jobs you had to endure (or even may be enduring right now). What skills did you learn from just being faithful to that job? Perhaps you learned how not to manage a business from a bad boss or observed first-hand what can happen with careless leadership.

Today's verses describe what can happen to us when we love God—every detail in life can be used for something good. That means the awful stuff you went through, the tedious work, the stormy nights—all of those experiences can be woven together to produce good. You've been working on dream for a long time—whether you know it or not. You've gained valuable experience and insight just from the positions you've found yourself in. And if you are still in a place you'd rather not be, use this time to learn valuable lessons you won't need to learn when you're on your own and soaring as your own business owner.

Nothing is wasted when we trust God. Take stock of all you've learned.

Thank God for your lessons.

Inspiration

Then the Lord God formed the man of dust from the ground and breathed into his nostrils the breath of life, and the man became a living creature.

(Genesis 2:7, ESV)

In *Soar!*, I write a lot about inspiration. It is a requirement to begin a business and to stick with it. Inspiration can come in many forms; in fact, the thing that inspires you may not even be noticed by someone else. God amazingly created each of us differently and we are inspired by just as many different things.

The word *inspire* comes from the Latin *inspirare* and it means to blow or breathe life into something. It's the same word we find in the creation story in Genesis. When God created man, He picked up the dust off the ground and formed it into a human being. And once that human, Adam, was formed, God took his own breath and breathed into him, making the man to come to life.

I like to note that God formed Adam's body first. Then, God breathed into the body. It was a process. And we as entrepreneurs need to follow that process, too. We can be inspired by a situation and try to run with our inspiration, using all of our energy to make it work. However, we forget about the basics and the structure.

Even with inspiration—great inspiration—we can't forgo the steps needed to form a structure. You can't launch your start-up and not pay attention to how to manage day-to-day operations. You can't run off and hire people without figuring out your budget, without expenditures and projected income. It takes more than inspiration to run a business. Yes, inspiration can fuel your creativity and give you many awesome ideas, but don't bypass the formation of the business. Give careful thought and planning time to forming the ideas you have received inspiration to create. Honor the process.

What has inspired you?

You intended to harm me, but God intended it all for good. He brought me to this position so I could save the lives of many people. (Genesis 50:20, NLT)

While I applaud the concept of inspiration and recognize it is something all successful entrepreneurs have, I don't discount its need to work in tandem with innovation and other concepts. Inspiration alone can be short-lived and short circuit a business quickly. Inspiration fuels the dream, but so much more gets it running and even expanding.

Successful business leaders understand the importance of adapting to changing conditions—or even observing the conditions. They understand that what they start off with may not be what they ultimately end up with—and wisdom helps them go with what emerges.

Think of the numerous successful products that started off as something else. Coca-Cola started off as a cure for headaches, but it eventually turned into a beverage to enjoy over ice more than a medicine. And Viagra came about when chemists were working on a new heart medicine and discovered its other benefits. The company didn't make their inspiration for a new heart medicine stop them from allowing the formula to produce a pill that helped in other ways.

If we remember Joseph's story in Genesis, we can be inspired to trust God and to trust the process fueled by our inspiration. Everything may not look like it is working in the proper order, but it is. Joseph had a dream that his brothers would bow to him (Genesis 37:6-8). I'm sure when he was inspired by this dream, he had some situations in mind. But never in his wildest dreams did he think his life would turn out as it did. This young man went from being adorned in a coat of many colors as his father's favorite son to being sold into slavery and living in a foreign land. He was also falsely accused of a crime and thrown in jail. Yet, his dream came to pass—and the result was probably even bigger than he imagined.

When we see a different path than the one we "dreamed," we don't have to be afraid to pursue it. Sometimes what looks like harm—or a different dream—is really God's creative way of turning bad into good—or expanding our vision.

What are you dreaming about?

Do It Better

There's nothing new on this earth. Year after year it's the same old thing.

(Ecclesiastes 1:9, MSG)

I've heard several would-be entrepreneurs complain about not being creative enough to come up with an idea for a business, invention, or innovation. My response to them is, "No problem—just take something people want or need in your area and do it better than anyone else!"

You don't have to come up with original ideas to be successful. People need the same basic things—food and drink, shelter, clothing. And, people generally want the same things. The wise King Solomon put it best in Ecclesiastes when he proclaimed: "There's nothing new under the sun." He had taken time out to observe life and he concluded that it's pretty much the same each year after year. If it's been done once, it's been done again.

So with that in mind, don't be afraid to jump into the entrepreneurial game. And don't use the excuse that you have nothing new to contribute. What services do you use? What do you see people around you spending lots of money on? What isn't done to your liking? What displeases you most? Sometimes our passion isn't readily observed in what we like, but more so in what we dislike.

You may see a problem and can come up with the solution—and offer it to people who will be willing to pay you for it. You can take any product or service and improve on it. Start by thinking what would make you buy more or patronize a business more. Perhaps a special service catered to people like you. You can build upon another's business idea and make it better—or better serve a particular audience.

Don't let fear of duplicating a business stop you from being your own boss. There's always more room for a good business done even better.

What can you do better?

"Therefore keep watch, because you do not know on what day your Lord will come. But understand this: If the owner of the house had known at what time of night the thief was coming, he would have kept watch and would not have let his house be broken into. So you also must be ready, because the Son of Man will come at an hour when you do not expect him."   (Matthew 24:42-44, NIV)

Just like life, sometimes a business will get an unexpected shift, propelled by the undercurrent. It's not because of anything the owner has done; it's just that the weather has changed to his or her advantage. For example, when the talented singer Patti LaBelle decided to diversify and launch a new line of sweet potato pies, she had no idea how the brand could be hit by a windstorm, causing sales to go off the chart.

A super fan of Patti's inadvertently helped her out. James Wright posted a humorous three-minute video on YouTube demonstrating that eating the pies made him sing like Patti. This video, simply produced by a fan, went viral. Within a few days, it was viewed more than five million times. Patti's promotional team didn't come up with the idea, but her team and Walmart, the seller of the pies, benefited. The pies flew off the shelves, and Walmart, no doubt, had to change their production process to keep up with the unexpected high demand.

Now what would have happened if they were not equipped to increase production? A wonderful opportunity would have been wasted. No matter how great Wright's video was, customers needed to find the pies in the stores to purchase them.

And a good business leader knows the importance of staying ready. You can't predict every upswing or down swing in your business; but you can stay ready to make changes when and where needed—quickly.

When Jesus was telling his followers to be ready, he used a parable to let them know the importance of staying ready. Of course, if we knew what time of day or hour he was coming, we'd be prepared. But we do not know. So we need to stay prepared and stay ready.

How have you prepared for an upswing in your business?

The manager said to himself, "What shall I do now? My master is taking away my job. I'm not strong enough to dig, and I'm ashamed to beg—I know what I'll do so that, when I lose my job here, people will welcome me into their houses."

(Luke 16:3-4, NIV)

The word "shrewd" may not always evoke the most pleasant images, but a shrewd business person is often a wise and successful one.

A shrewd person does his or her homework. She studies the conditions on the ground. He takes data and interprets it for today as well as to make educated predictions about the future. For example, opening a high-end dress boutique for young professional women in an area filled with factories may not be a wise decision; or choosing to open a restaurant that caters to young crowds in a retirement community just might not cut it. You need to study the lay of the land when making choices.

That's one reason I like the parable in Luke. It shows a manager who is thinking, perhaps only after he is threatened with losing his job, but it is better later than never to be shrewd and handle your business. This manager realizes the conditions around him are changing—he's about to lose his job. So, what's next? He takes account of his surroundings and realizes he can gain favor with the people he currently serves. He allows them to reduce their debt to his boss, putting himself in a positive position with them. He thinks they will remember his help and grant him help in return. The man's boss commends him for being shrewd.

Some people wonder if this parable is advocating being dishonest. But I think its point is to remind us to be wise and sharp as we run our affairs in this world and for God's Kingdom. The shrewd person is a wise person who is ever-observant of the circumstances.

Are you paying attention to your surroundings?

A Valuable Asset

[Wisdom shouts:] But all who listen to me will live in peace, untroubled by fear of harm.

(Proverbs 1:33, NLT)

A wise entrepreneur knows that one of the most valuable assets around is the competition. You can learn a great deal by studying your competition—really studying. I'm not suggesting you make notes about how you're so much better than the person selling a similar product or service as you, but you put on your researcher cap and really examine your competition.

I suggest experiencing your competition just as a customer would, remembering to take unbiased note of all the details, from your first contact until you conclude your transaction. You should notice how helpful and friendly the service was; how could this help you improve the way you or your team interacts with customers? How can this help you train your employees?

I'd even go as far as to try to talk with owners of businesses that have failed. What didn't work can serve as priceless information for you. Don't be afraid to ask; people love to share their experiences. Ask what they wish they would have known before they started their venture or before its decline. And if you can talk with a business owner who is still operating—especially profitably—ask the same question. You may be able to come up with a way to help each other.

Listening and observing others is a wise decision. When you listen to wisdom, you can live in peace and you don't have to worry about harm. Every mistake does not have to be yours to make. Let wisdom teach you to learn from others. You only have to listen.

Whose business are you studying?

The islands have seen it and fear; the ends of the earth tremble.

They approach and come forward; they help each other and say to their companions, "Be strong!"

(Isaiah 41:5-6, NIV)

Your competition is a valuable resource for several other reasons. When you have competition, it forces you to bring your A game—if you want to be at the top. You don't need to avoid interacting with your competition; you already know you can learn a lot from each other—after all, you have the same goals and the same customers.

While you're not going to simply imitate each other, you can learn methods and mistakes that will save you valuable time and money. You can also learn what sets you apart from your competition, which can give you sound bites to use in your marketing.

And don't forget, every business needs to be able to refer customers to others when they are at their capacity or cannot serve the customer at that time. No one wants to turn business away, but when that happens, being able to point your customer in another direction makes you look good. In the end, you are helping the customer, who may return to you at another time—or share the experience with another customer.

I appreciate it when a hotel or restaurant is filled and the hosts share a similar alternative restaurant with me. It gives me more options when my first choice is not available. And at the end of the day, I really just want a comfortable hotel room or a good meal.

Are you bringing your A game?

> Don't copy the behavior and customs of this world, but let God transform you into
> a new person by changing the way you think. Then you will learn to know God's
> will for you, which is good and pleasing and perfect.   (Romans 12:2, NLT)

Successful business people are always thinking. And those of us who live by faith know the importance of letting God renew our minds. When we rely on God for renewal, we can think of ideas that may not have ever come to us. Relying on God leads to refreshing and rejuvenating our minds—and finding peace. That's a good sign.

Don't let the busy-ness of running your venture drive you to burn out. Remember the importance of being renewed. Some people like vacations where they unplug. Others take intentional Sabbath rests once a week where they do not carry a phone or check email.

In order to completely let go for a period, you need to have good processes in place as well as trained and skilled people you trust. There's nothing like leaving your business to someone you don't believe is capable of handling issues. You won't rest even though you are "off" or not actively engaging in the operations during that time.

Other ways to renew your mind are networking with like-minded business people, participating in your favorite hobby, and spending time with your family and friends. They can help you gain perspective, which will probably help you make better decisions when you do return to your business.

How do you renew your mind?

Don't Be Swift

I have seen something else under the sun: The race is not to the swift.

(Ecclesiastes 9:11a, NIV)

The story of Daedalus offers a cautionary tale about succeeding too quickly—and quite frankly about not listening.

When Daedalus thought of the brilliant plan to create wings so that he and his son, Icarus, could fly out of the complex labyrinth that was impossible to walk through, he used the materials available to him to create their wings, beeswax and sticks. Daedalus knew the wax could melt if they flew to close to the sun—so he told Icarus to be careful near the sun.

Well, Icarus allowed his excitement to eclipse his father's warning. When he realized that he could fly, he wanted to soar high and fast. He allowed his passion and newfound freedom to override practicality. And as you can guess, the young Icarus didn't heed his father's advice and maintain an altitude that he could sustain; he flew high and fast and the sun burned his waxed wings. Icarus couldn't keep flying. He crashed into the sea and drowned.

Just like Icarus, many business owners get excited when they start to fly. They don't always monitor their altitude and take off—sometimes making promises they can't possible fulfill. In *Soar!*, I describe what happened to this small printing company that employed many homeless men and women. We wanted to utilize their business and ordered a print job for some promotional materials for an upcoming event.

While the director was thrilled, her enthusiasm could not make up for the lack of organizational resources required to fulfill this order. Despite the good intentions and significant donations of people, this venture did not last long. It dissolved the following year, and I was not surprised.

Enthusiasm can make some people bite off more than they are ready to chew. A wise business person assesses the situation and provides a realistic assessment—whether that is to employ the help of someone who can manage a larger order or anticipate other changes to get the job done. Enthusiasm doesn't make you fly higher than you can sustain. People are counting on your service, not just your zeal. Know what you can deliver.

How do you maintain a sustainable altitude?

Study to shew thyself approved unto God, a workman that needeth not to be ashamed, rightly dividing the word of truth.   (2 Timothy 2:15, KJV)

Most entrepreneurs begin with a vision or a dream; they want to have a business or provide a service based off of their dream and goal. They have a hustler's mentality—a mindset that says they will do whatever they need to do to make their dream a reality. They long to be their own boss and call the shots. And while you definitely need a special drive to succeed, drive alone is not enough.

If you want to soar, you will need to shift from a hustler to a business leader. And depending on your experience, that may mean studying—whether as an apprentice, an intern, a student, a mentee, or all of these plus some.

Regardless of your gifts and skills and your drive, you don't know all there is to know about your business. You may have the best ideas and the most determination, but you also need the wisdom to know what you don't have and go after it. You need to acquire new skills—business skills—that help you think long-term and see the big picture rather than just your immediate goals.

You need to know how to hone your hustle to make your business work for you. You may start off with the idea and the drive, but you've got to put in more to create a successful business. And you will need to study business—in some capacity—to prove yourself as someone who is ready to fly.

How are you improving yourself and business?

For the love of money is a root of all kinds of evil, and in their eagerness to be rich some have wandered away from the faith and pierced themselves with many pains.   (1 Timothy 6:10, NRSV)

There's nothing wrong with wanting to make money. Businesses need to make a profit to succeed. And entrepreneurs want to succeed financially as much as anyone. But be careful if making loads of money is your primary reason for starting a business. I think if money is your primary motivation, you have already limited how high you will fly. You may be able to get your business off the ground, but at some point the fatigue from your journey will wear you down. Your hustle has to be about more than money.

What will keep you going is your motivation; many want to create something they can call their own and add their unique twist to it. They are driven by a desire to do something better, bigger, or differently. Money is a great by-product and it can be used to enhance, advance, or expand. Money may be important, but so is customer service, quality products, and innovation. When you are only concerned about money, you will cut corners to make short-term gains and end up hurting people and your product in the long run.

There's no wonder scripture says the *love* of money is the root of evil. When you are driven to make more, you lose sight of the big picture. The dollar becomes your focus and can become your god. Be careful, because eventually, you will do anything for more money.

Check your motivations—and make sure you're in this game to win more than big profits. Be led by your desire to do better and provide better for others. And trust that with hard work, wisdom, perseverance, and the goal to be the best at what you do, money will come.

What's your motivation?

For wisdom will enter your heart, and knowledge will be pleasant to your soul.

(Proverbs 2:10, NIV)

Finding your potential customers requires you ask plenty of questions. And as soon as you answer one question, often two more will pop up in its place.

To demonstrate how knowing your customer can help you hone in on your market and improve your product or services, I'll use an example I discuss in *Soar!*

Let's say you make a mean pound cake. It is delicious and you've even been told that you should sell it. So, you set out to sell your pound cakes. When asked what your core customer base is, you might respond with, "Everyone loves pound cake, right? So I need to target as many people as possible. Everyone is my target audience so I'm starting off as an online business."

While your optimism is impressive, this type of thinking won't make you successful. Can everyone find you online? Does everyone have the means and are they inclined to order pound cake they haven't tasted? It's imperative that you do further research and thinking to find the right customers.

You should ask: Is pound cake really viable when everyone else seems to be doing well with cupcakes? What makes cupcakes sell well and how does that compare to what you are offering? How many flavors of pound cake will you offer? Will the taste and quality of your cakes be impacted by shipping? What will you need to adjust when shipping? How will you ship and what is the cost of shipping? Is shipping cost effective? Can customers make special requests?

We could go on with more and more questions, but as you can see, there's plenty to think about when finding your target customer and positioning your product to suit their needs. When defining your audience, resist the temptation to think everyone is a customer. You want to have enough information to truly know who you serve and who you want to serve. Then you can cater your business to fit their specific need.

Who is your customer? What do they want or need from you?

You need to persevere so that when you have done the will of God, you will receive
what he has promised.   (Hebrews 10:36. NIV)

I've warned against being only motivated by money when entering the wild,
wild west world of entrepreneurship. It's important to check your motives
and know why you want to enter into this space.

If your personal vision is to have more autonomy, freedom, and flexibility,
then creating your own just might be for you. However, I should warn you: you
will probably work harder and longer in your own venture than as someone
else's employee. You will trade in a sense of "security" that can come with a reg-
ular paycheck for freedom and the thrill of creating something that is all your
own. It can be a positive trade-off, but again, be sure to check your motives.

Some people may think that setting their own hours and being their own
boss means that they can retire to a tropical island as soon as their business
becomes profitable. But that's not how it works. Successful entrepreneurs I
know work harder than ever because they are pursuing their dream; they have
more at stake and they want to succeed. They often have working vacations
rather than breaking away for two weeks, but because they are driven to succeed, they do what they have to do.

And to be honest, just like with most things, the entrepreneurial flight can
be harder on minorities or those in underserved communities. The struggle
is real, but we have to endure. Success comes to those who keep pressing and
working—despite the obstacles. Success doesn't trickle down; it springs up
from inside a heart that beats to the drum of creativity until a goal is obtained—
and another one is set and obtained. It's how you keep soaring.

So, as you evaluate your motivations for venturing on your own, ask yourself if you have what it takes to keep pressing and endure this race. If you do,
many fulfilled promises await you.

Do you have what it takes to endure?

> Go now, write it before them on a tablet, and inscribe it in a book, so that it may be
> for the time to come as a witness forever.   (Isaiah 30:8, NRSV)

Turning your dream into a reality will require a strategic plan and the resourcefulness to use the materials available to you. And one of your resources is the written record. You can use a business plan or an unstructured document on your computer, but I think it is important to write down what you are planning to do—and revisit your strategy often.

Writing down your goal has power. It can serve as a record for time to come. When you perhaps forget why you're doing what you are doing, you can review your written record. When you are trying to decide if a new opportunity will yield another path toward your dream, you can review your strategy.

While writing down a plan doesn't mean you have to follow it to the letter—or even forgo writing an addendum—having your plan in writing creates a concrete guide. It gives you an outlet to process your thoughts and get them out of your head. You can share the plan with trusted advisors who can offer valuable input.

When you grow, you may adjust your plan—just like a pilot adjusts with certain weather conditions. You can use the force and direction of the wind to your advantage if you have the tools to forecast the conditions ahead of you. Use the wind to propel you in the air and to help your business soar to new heights!

Have you written a plan?

Thus says the Lord God of Israel: Write all the words that I have spoken to you in a book.

(Jeremiah 30:2, MEV)

I am always surprised when a budding entrepreneur approaches me for advice or even an investment and the person does not have a business plan for me to review. When I ask for the plan, some share that it's in their head. But, I can't read your mind or see what's in your mind. I know some things can happen quickly and business can take off without a written plan. But it is in the best interest of the owner to carve out the time to write a vision and plan as early as possible in the business venture.

Yes, your ideas for your business will begin in your brain. That's good as a first step. But at some point before you build your business, you need to build your plan—on paper. When you first start to write your business plan, it can feel like you're talking out loud on paper or on your computer screen. You may add, change, erase, revise, and refine your plan.

Your business plan tells others—as well as yourself—what you intend to do and how your business will look and function. It tells you where you are going and how you plan to get there.

Think about the importance of a blueprint to an architect. The builder doesn't just start putting together concrete or bricks or wood to create a structure. No, design plans are drawn up and put on paper. The client needs to approve them before any building actually happens. The design plans include detailed research taking into account weight loads, heating concerns, functionality, and aesthetics. If it is planned right with the pencil, it will be built right with steel.

It's the same with your business plan. It serves as a blueprint. You can function better when you have a written plan to refer to, and anyone seriously considering investing their resources will be able to study your plan and assess their risks. Your business plan is a way to share your destination and how you plan to get there.

Do you have a blueprint for your business?

This is what the Lord, the God of Israel, says: "Write down for the record everything I have said to you, Jeremiah."   (Jeremiah 30:2, NLT)

When creating your business plan, remember that it should represent your business' uniqueness, your personal passion, your professional advantages, and your clients' sensibilities. You can use templates—and there are many to choose from—but make sure you customize the plan to your industry, field, and audience. For example, a business plan for a neighborhood beauty salon will look different from a plan for a technical consulting business or a plan for selling your hand knitting online.

Your plan can be from one page to many pages, depending on what message you have to convey. Some chose to offer a skeletal overview of their business while others make a more full-bodied elaboration. But all plans—regardless of their size or form—should remain works in progress, always available to be adjusted, adapted, and updated depending on the weather conditions around your industry.

As you start to formalize your plan, ask yourself a few questions. Answering these will give you the needed information for your plan. I'll explain more about each question in subsequent parts of this devotion (and in the book) to help you draft your plan—or enhance what you've already created.

Ask yourself: What are you selling or what problem are you solving? Who needs what you are offering? Why do they need it? How will your business operate? Where will your business operate? When will you start your business?

Answer the questions of what, who, why, how, where, and when for your business.

This is what the Lord, the God of Israel, says: "Write in a book all the words I have spoken to you…"

(Jeremiah 30:2, NIV)

After you have thought through the answers to the who, what, when, where, why, and how of your business, you are ready to create your plan. But wait, what if you are not particularly fond of writing long, detailed responses and you don't think it is best to hire someone more comfortable with writing to help you?

Perhaps your business can benefit from another form of business plan. Everything does not have to follow the same format. Some business owners can convey their visions much better through graphics, charts, and pictures. They may opt to pull together a PowerPoint style presentation that shows more than tells what they intend to do with their business.

Or perhaps a video will tell your story better—especially if your business will utilize videography more than print. For example, if you have a plan for a firm that specializes in creating videos for social media, creating a plan via video is not only a way to demonstrate your plans but an actual demonstration of your capabilities. Consider posting your video to YouTube or recording a podcast. If done well, these creative forms of business plans can provide all the specific information one usually finds in a written plan.

All plans should include an overview of your mission, or an executive summary; a description of the atmosphere you intend to operate in; market analysis and competitive strategies; operational logistics; financials; and how you will know you've met your goals or metrics.

In general, when crafting your plan, do what works best for you and your business. And have something tangible you can leave with potential investors and customers.

How does your business plan look?

Perfect Conditions

We all stumble in many ways… (James 3:2a, NIV)

As you create your business plan and prepare to take flight, the idealist in you may be tempted to believe if you do all of your homework and gauge the conditions accurately, you can succeed without trouble. While I encourage you to do all the preparation work possible, I also invite you to remember that you don't need perfect conditions to have success. In fact, the nature of beginning any venture brings along with it uncertainty and levels of imperfection.

Remember the Wright brothers started working on their flying machine in a bicycle shop in Dayton, Ohio. The idea environment for what they were building didn't exist yet. Working in that shop provided them with most of the raw ingredients they needed. And they kept working on their invention.

Start-ups often resemble the start of a marriage; in order for it to be successful, you have to make adjustments and accommodations for the new dynamics. But that of course shouldn't stop people from getting married and it shouldn't stop you from launching your business.

In fact, expecting some dysfunction can help you modify your expectations. You can address potential pitfalls and resolutions in your business plan and keep on the lookout for new solutions.

What you create may not be exactly as outlined in your plan; use the dysfunction to improve your business and your plans. Mistakes, errors, and disappointments are necessary ingredients. So avoid trying to get things perfect and exact and focus on what you can learn for improvement.

Are you expecting perfection?

For we are God's masterpiece. He has created us anew in Christ Jesus, so we can
do the good things he planned for us long ago.   (Ephesians 2:10, NLT)

I believe taking responsibility for your own success is vital if you want to be a successful entrepreneur. If you were raised like I was, you knew that your responsibility as a young adult was to leave your parents' nest and test your wings; you were expected to go on to school and graduate in hope of landing a life-long position. Or perhaps you learned a trade and used it at a job that you worked for forty or fifty years and received a gold watch at retirement. That was then.

Now, we are in a whole new realm. With a shrinking middle class, we need to look within to find the creativity God has created in us all to pull ourselves up as best we can. While everyone won't be an entrepreneur, those who are— and are successful—will use their God-given talents to meet a need and produce a business.

Some of us just don't have the strength and stamina to stay perched in our present situations, working at the same job for the long haul. Some of us have gone as far as possible with our present wings and we need a paradigm shift in our vision to adjust life's flight plan.

What our parents modeled was acute wisdom for their time; but now we can't fulfill our destiny by merely imitating our parents' models. There may be some practical advice and parts of their model we can use, but there's also a larger world awaiting those who will launch out and fly. Use your faith— and remember you are a masterpiece; but not just any masterpiece. You were designed with your skills, likes and dislikes by the ultimate Artist. Use what God has put inside of you to stretch out and do something new.

Do you have the faith to create a new path?

I applied my heart to what I observed and learned a lesson from what I saw.

(Proverbs 24:32, NIV)

If you want your business to succeed, you must become a keen student and observant detective when it comes to leveraging contact with your target audience. I use an entire chapter in *Soar!* to exalt the amazing benefits of e-commerce. If you have a business, I'm sure you've already explored the numerous ways e-commerce can help your business—even if it is not an online business, you can utilize the web and social media to enhance it.

However, no matter how great your banner ad is or how clever your hashtags are, your target market still needs to be reached. You have to figure out where and how to connect with current and potential customers. And customers are looking for something from you, too, online. Businesses clients trust and value three things: consistency, quality, and adaptability. They're all part of your brand and should be seamlessly translated online.

You probably have less than three seconds to keep a person's attention online, so make sure your message matches what you are offering and is quickly understood and memorable. And you want to assure that your brand's messaging matches the level of quality of your business. Each message should deliver and convey excellence. If people see misspelled words or sloppy graphics (or bad pictures) on your advertising, they can assume details do not matter to you and skip on over your services.

And remaining flexible and adaptable means you can change with the needs of your customers. Nothing is worse than an outdated product or service; when you remain adaptable, you pay attention to the winds and shift with the needs. Shifting doesn't mean you are unpredictable or stable; it means you are keen, observant, and customer-focused—a winning combination.

How is your online presence?

A faithful person will be richly blessed.   (Proverbs 28:20a, NIV)

In *Soar!*, I talk about how e-commerce has put the "e" in "easy." The Internet, technology, and shipping have not only made shopping easy; they have all made owning a business a little more accessible.

E-commerce can be attractive to those who want to have a business to subsidize their existing income, or perhaps to those who want to ease into the entrepreneurial game with little start-up costs or risks. E-commerce may be a great option for those having to care for ailing parents or young children. You can be at home operating a business and making profits.

A lot of times, you don't have to decide between a brick-and-mortar business and e-commerce. You may not be ready for a physical site, but you definitely can offer your goods and services online pretty quickly and easily. You can use the online business to test products, get a feel for how business can be or as a viable and long-term platform.

Remember to utilize social media to your advantage by linking your site to all of the social media outlets your potential customer uses. It's the easiest way to be open twenty-four hours around the world. You can service customers with products, seminars, and exercise training while you are still in your pajamas.

Running your online business also requires less money than a physical business. You usually won't have to have office space, leases, insurance or payroll taxes. E-commerce has become the fastest growing segment of our economy in recent years. You, too, can have a piece of that pie.

Have you considered an e-commerce business?

... there will be a time for every activity, a time for every deed.

(Ecclesiastes 3:17b, NIV)

Hiring is a big part of successfully running a business. And hiring the right people can make your venture take off. I believe the old adage "hire slowly and fire quickly" holds some truth. Doing your due diligence and thoroughly reviewing a person's qualifications (slow hiring) *before* you make an offer and invite them on your team can save you a world of trouble later. Find out if their past work history, education, and performance fits what you need. Ask questions of the potential employee as well as their references, and listen carefully to the answers.

Many entrepreneurs rush to hire people when their business experiences growth. They want to fill a position quickly to meet a need and continue to grow. Instead of relying on temp agencies to fill in these holes, leaders sometimes run out and try to fill the seat with permanent employees. This type of quick hiring usually doesn't result in employees who will go the long haul with the company. Instead, they often leave soon or need to leave even sooner and you're stuck having to go through the hiring process again.

Taking your time to make sure a potential candidate not only can do the job but is also a good fit for your operation is critical. You want team members who understand your vision and can run with it. You want people who can do the job that is available and offer even more—gifts and skills that may be helpful in growing your business in the future. When employees feel their skills are needed and encouraged, they grow as people as well as team members. Your company becomes a nurturing place for their development and you get more than an employee—you get a blooming flower who will hopefully add value to your team.

What is your strategy for hiring?

Due Diligence

As iron sharpens iron, so a friend sharpens a friend.   (Proverbs 27:17, NLT)

When I first started out as an entrepreneur, I had the misfortune of having to deal with a frivolous lawsuit against my company. A contractor had hoped to cash in on my rapidly accelerating ascent as a businessman and pastor.

I didn't settle. We went all the way to court. In court, however, I was very impressed with the accuser's attorney. He wasn't impressive because of his eloquence or glamor. His appearance was professional but not flashy. There wasn't anything slick about him at all—but he knew the law and had a clear strategy for presenting his client's case against me and my business. He was well-prepared and represented his client exceptionally.

After the case was resolved and the dust settled, I called that attorney and invited him to lunch, where I offered him a job. He, no doubt, was surprised, but I had done my due diligence. I had researched his background and past experience and it lined up with his impressive performance in court. I had asked questions and found out that he seemed like a great fit for my company. I wanted him on my team. I recognized his strong capabilities. He accepted the offer and went on to represent my businesses and me for more than a decade.

Building the best team possible may require you to look in unexpected places. When you see someone sharp who may fit in well with your organization, research his or her history and get acquainted. Strong minds sharpen other strong minds, just like iron sharpens iron. Find your team members who will bring out the best in each other.

How do you find sharp iron for your team?

All in the Family

An offended friend is harder to win back than a fortified city. Arguments separate friends like a gate locked with bars.   (Proverbs 18:19, NLT)

While I suggest entrepreneurs hire cautiously and take their time to find the right people for their team, I especially suggest caution when employing family members and close friends. I have employed family members with a certain degree of success, but there are some things I always do when bringing a relative onboard my team.

First, I make sure expectations are discussed and clearly defined. I then ask them if they are able to deliver what is expected. I give them a chance to think about what I'm looking for and evaluate if they are up to the challenge. I also try to make sure I share that their role in the company may expand or possibly be eliminated depending on the weather conditions; this way, if anything comes up, they will know it is not personal but rather strictly business.

Then, when they are on board, I try to separate my family role from our business relationship. I may be father or uncle or cousin, but when we are working, I am manager, boss, etc. They are the provider of whatever role or service they have been hired to perform. When we are working, we are not discussing family issues, and when we are at a family dinner or gathering, we are not talking about the business. Our roles are separate and different.

I also ask the relative to avoid discussing company or work-related issues with other family members and vow to do the same. And I try to make sure they understand that our relationship as family is more important than the business so if one needs to be dissolved, it will be our business relationship. You can replace an employee; you cannot replace a family member.

There are great risks employing family, but on the flip side, there probably isn't anything better than sharing the success and profits of your business with those you love. So, before you employee family, make sure it is worth the risk.

What are your thoughts on employing family?

> Understand this, my dear brothers and sisters: You must all be quick to listen, slow to speak, and slow to get angry. (James 1:19, NLT)

In *Soar!*, I tell the story of a New York retailer in a high end men's clothing shop. I noticed how attentive the gentleman was to each customer, but without hovering or being pushy, and was honest in his opinions regardless of how they might tilt the potential purchase. He treated everyone with courtesy, respect, and genuine interest. When I realized he was the owner of the store, I asked his secret.

He told me, "With every customer, I ask myself what I can do to make sure they have a pleasant experience that will make them want to come back. Even if they don't buy something today, how can I influence them to return when they need to purchase something here in the future? Obviously, it's not the same for every customer so the real key is *listening* to and *engaging* with what each customer tells you they need."

He had the secret. Most people want to be heard. Even if they are not buying anything at the time, the owner wanted them to feel so special that they would remember the shop and the experience there—and they would return when ready to make a purchase or even share how they felt with others, who in turn might patronize the store.

It is true: People want to be heard. They are not only purchasing items. They are purchasing experiences. What do you offer other than your product? The customers at the men's shop surely liked the product, but I'm sure they returned because they received more than a suit or tie. They received an experience where they were heard. Perhaps the teenager received confidence for the interview along with his suit; the woman shopping for her husband learned how to make him feel even more special and the businessman purchasing cuff links also received affirmation. Not everything can be purchased; some things are experienced and offered without charge—but those very things may bring in more sales.

What do customers experience when they utilize your business?

Your End Game, Part 1

Do you not know that in a race all the runners run, but only one gets the prize?
Run in such a way as to get the prize.   (1 Corinthians 9:24, NIV)

It may sound silly to ask you to think about the end game of your business—after all you are planning to build a long-running successful business, I'm sure. But thinking about the end at the beginning can yield many benefits. Knowing where you're going—or you'd like to go—can help you build for the long haul and run this race to gain the prize of building a successful business.

Knowing what you intend to build can help you make choices with more accuracy, efficiency, and intentionality. Think about the way real estate investors work. Before they even purchase a property, they know they intend to flip it—to renovate, remodel, and redesign it and sell it for a profit. Therefore, they are better able to ignore their own personal styles and tastes and go for more generic, neutral colors and décor. This way the property can appeal to a broader audience.

The investors may also choose materials that are modestly priced in order to keep their costs down. Or they can even buy materials in bulk. They select the items based on what they will be able to use in other properties. They are thinking about the end game (to sell the home for a profit) every step of the way.

While your vision will morph as you grow, there is still much value in thinking ahead. You may ask yourself: Is this a business you hope to pass on to your children and grandchildren? Or is this a business you'd like to liquidate in ten years? Are you looking to be bought out by a large competitor after a certain time? Or are you launching this business to create or supplement retirement income? The answers to these questions can help your decisions today.

Don't just run. Run with your prize—and end game—in mind.

What is the ideal end game for your business?

Everyone who competes in the games goes into strict training. They do it to get a
crown that will not last, but we do it to get a crown that will last forever.

(1 Corinthians 9:25, NIV)

There's plenty to consider when envisioning your end game. Even if you
expect your business to outlast you, it's important to think about its end
now. When you think about where you are going and what to do when you get
there, it makes things less confusing when the time comes to make the decision. It's akin to couples signing prenuptial agreements before they are married. They know it is easier to think of how to practically dissolve the union
while they are still happy. While they hope the day will never come when they
have to end their marriage, having a clear plan written out can save a great deal
of headache and surprises later.

As you think about your end game, ask yourself what would make you sell
your business. What conditions and terms would you need? Would you want
to keep your name on the business or be closely associated with it? Would you
want to remain involved in some capacity or would you want anyone from your
staff to be involved?

Think through how you would want to handle issues around your marketing slogans, proprietary products, etc., can save you considerable time, energy,
and money down the road should the opportunity arise. Anticipating what
could happen can help you avoid some conflicts down the road—and it just
might help you sleep better at night, too.

How do you want to deal with the end?

Though one may be overpowered, two can defend themselves. A cord of three strands is not quickly broken.   (Ecclesiastes 4:12, NIV)

Building and sustaining a viable business can sometimes make you isolated. You want to pour your time and energy into nurturing and growing your creative venture. Yet, a wise entrepreneur knows that he or she is really only as strong as the network. And successful business leaders are always working on expanding and extending their network. Those who truly want to soar make sure they have relationships with people other than customers, employees, coworkers and competitors. They look outside of their box and comfort zone to learn from others.

Cultivating relationships with a wide spectrum of people with different professional and personal endeavors can ignite your creativity in ways that working with those who are like you just can't. You can find motivation and inspiration from others, which in turn can make you stronger. And like a three strand cord, you won't be easily broken or separated; there can be great power in working with, learning from, and networking with others.

I have grown from my encounters with a wide and diverse population of thinkers, artists, leaders, ministers, inventors, and innovators. We may appear to have nothing in common, but once we began sharing, my mind runs in new directions looking for transferable traits and methods. My partnerships and networks help me to replenish my creativity and hone my problem-solving skills. And I hope I, in turn, can ignite passions to help others grow their ventures so we can all soar and make valuable contributions to society.

How broad is your network?

This makes for harmony among the members, so that all the members care for each other. If one part suffers, all the parts suffer with it, and if one part is honored, all the parts are glad.   (1 Corinthians 12:25-26, NLT)

I like to remind the business leaders I talk to that they can't forget the "net" in networking. Nets are woven strands of roped fibers designed to contain certain items while letting others pass through. Nets provide a flexible filter to help anglers, athletes, and entomologists snare their fish, field goals, and fireflies.

Networks can help you get your job done, too. As one person, you are limited by a finite amount of time, energy, and ability. You have only two hands and can only accomplish what those two hands can do. By assembling the best team possible from your network you can support, sustain, and soar with your new venture.

It can be tempting to try to launch your business by yourself—or to try to take it to the next level alone. But you are not Superman or Wonder Woman; don't limit your superpowers by isolating yourself! You will crash and burn quickly. Defying gravity and reaching your destination is a journey and it can't be taken alone.

Utilize those around you. Make connections with people who have strong skills—even skills that are different than yours. The strongest, most dynamic resources are often built on strands of connectivity that cross barriers and integrate diverse perspectives.

Do you rely on your network?

A gentle answer turns away wrath, but a harsh word stirs up anger.

(Proverbs 15:1, NIV)

In his book *The 21 Irrefutable Laws of Leadership*, John Maxwell emphasizes that leadership is predicated on influence. Leadership cannot be exercised in isolation. Your influence needs to be exercised on a daily basis.

Entrepreneurial influence is more than making a pitch or completing a sale. It is about how you brand yourself, promote yourself, and market your products and services. Your influence is reflected in relationships and how you interact with others. It is measured by how well you can influence those around you in constructive, consistent, and coherent ways.

Influence is not only in the message you communicate but *how* you communicate it. True influence actively listens and keenly observes all those around you and how they interact with you.

Influence also makes you control your response to all you confront. You know you need to exercise self-discipline many times so you don't become riled up and emotionally distracted, which can create even more problems. You find ways of expressing your point of view without undermining your ultimate objective. You learn to choose your words carefully—as well as the timing in which you utter those words. Gentle words can change the atmosphere for the better while harsh words can create chaos.

How are you using your influence?

Avoid Turbulence

How much better to get wisdom than gold, to get insight rather than silver!

(Proverbs 16:16, NIV)

S killed pilots, just like wise entrepreneurs, know how to avoid turbulence before they feel it.

First of all, their experience has taught them how turbulence feels. They've been through enough storms to know the conditions that occur before the storm. No lesson has been wasted. So, they use experience as their teacher and learn to recognize the telltale signs of trouble ahead based on wind speed, weather patterns, and altitude. And when they see these signs, they make quick decisions to avert them.

The best leaders learn to avoid needless challenges. They know some challenges will take them by surprise and they will to address them, but for those that are unnecessary, they know to avoid them and save their energy. They manage the situation before it develops into a full-blown crisis.

One of the ways to avert these crises is to think through the various possibilities and permutations of your business process. That's why knowing the business inside out, knowing the business plan inside out, and being a keen observer and lifelong learner are so critical to all who want to be successful. It is amazing how some problems can be avoided with a little precautionary work and foresight. A little insight can save you a great deal of money, time, and energy.

Can you identify turbulence before it occurs?

Timing

For everything there is a season, a time for every activity under heaven.

(Ecclesiastes 3:1, NLT)

When you start your new venture—or even expand a part of your business—it can be very tempting to turn to social media and tweet or post about it. We live in the type of society where we think we need to seize the opportunity to get the message out as frequently and as quickly as possible if we want to penetrate the market and capture public attention.

But, I often suggest to entrepreneurs that they consider timing when making such announcements. I'm not talking about knowing what time the most potential clients are on social media and timing your posts to hit then (although that isn't a bad strategy); but I think it is much more important to ensure that your venture has been tried and tested before launching a full blown marketing and promotional strategy. You don't want to fail because you've focused more on promoting your venture than testing and improving the business itself. There's almost nothing worse than having plenty of customers and a sub-par product still filled with bugs and errors.

Some entrepreneurs operate like someone who is in love, but they are really infatuated with the idea of being in love; the entrepreneur isn't really passionate about the product she offers as much as she is with being an entrepreneur—and wanting to get the word out. Getting your name out in front of people does not make you a successful business owner.

You don't want to crash and burn because you haven't taken the time to ensure your product is ready for prime time. Just as good pilots know to warm up engines before taking off at full speed, wise entrepreneurs know to focus on their product and processes before promotion. Test-marketing, focus groups, beta groups are all ways to test the products and continue to work on the process before engaging large crowds. As the Bible says, for everything there is a season.

Know what time it is.

Follow the Order

But everything should be done in a fitting and orderly way.

(1 Corinthians 14:40, NIV)

I love the story of the Wright brothers, as I use it throughout *Soar!* to demonstrate essential truths about entrepreneurship. Did you know that once the brothers got their plane off the ground, they kept refining their invention? They stabilized its pitch, improved control, and tested maneuverability. When they launched their first plane at Kitty Hawk, they didn't even have a press conference or a public celebration. No, they returned to their home in Ohio and continued to work. Their ultimate goal was not just to fly but also to maximize their invention's potential. You see, they knew what they wanted and they were patient and diligent enough to keep going until they got it. They worked in order and waited patiently for everything to line up.

The brothers worked in relative obscurity to prevent others from copying their designs. And even when they had a practical model in 1905, they stored it for two years. They wanted to have the patent for their invention even before they went out and secured buyers. When they received their patent in 1906, the brothers envisioned many possibilities for their inventions—including military usage. They wanted to demonstrate the flight machine for the U.S. and French governments. Negotiations were tricky however because the governments refused to offer contracts until they saw the demonstrations while the Wright brothers refused to have demonstrations without contracts. Eventually, all sides agreed to issue contracts that wouldn't be finalized until the after the demonstrations.

After demonstrations and further improvements, the brothers from Dayton, Ohio, became known for creating a revolutionary machine that would forever transform transportation. They not only gave us airplanes, they showed us how following a process and not forgoing order can bring about desirable results. Their method requires patience and wisdom, but it can lead to success.

What order do you need to follow?

Dear brothers and sisters, when troubles of any kind come your way, consider it an opportunity for great joy. For you know that when your faith is tested, your endurance has a chance to grow. So let it grow, for when your endurance is fully developed, you will be perfect and complete, needing nothing.

(James 1:2-4, NLT)

Persevering and learning to solve problems is essential to the success of an entrepreneur. Why? Because most wisdom is gained through experience. You learn from your mistakes; and you learn from the process of running your business and creating your product.

In *Soar!*, I compare this wisdom-gaining process to driving a car. You can read a textbook and learn all of the rules written in the handbook; you can learn all about your car from the owner's manual, but until you actually drive—for several hours—you don't really know how to drive. And the only way to become a master driver is to drive—and keep driving.

Experience produces characteristics that can only be gained through being on the job—that's why it is called experience. The more you encounter, the more you learn. Even when you run into issues or problems, you are learning. That's why James exalts Christians to consider troubles as a chance for great joy! Not many of us stand and cheer on troubles in our life; but if we remember to see trouble as an opportunity to help us grow and mature, we just might have a shout when we see trouble coming.

The more issues you have to deal with in your business, the more you will learn. And the more experienced you will become. James calls these types of people "perfect and complete, needing nothing." Mature people are filled with wisdom—gained from experience. They've seen the ups and downs—and have developed the perseverance to endure. Experience is a great teacher.

Enjoy the process of learning through trials.

Be patient, therefore, beloved, until the coming of the Lord. The farmer waits for
the precious crop from the earth, being patient with it until it receives the early
and the late rains.

(James 5:7, NRSV)

Entrepreneurs are like improv performers, or at least they should be. A
successful entrepreneur has learned to improvise during crisis. During
these times, they hone in on valuable tools such as: preparation, engagement,
resourcefulness, and creativity to come up with solutions that will help them
keep their businesses soaring. To withstand—and push past—the inevitable
crisis in a business, you must employ patience with the season you find yourself
in. This requires being flexible and adaptable to the conditions around you.

It's like the farmer described in today's verse. Farmers understand the
timing—as well as the conditions—needed to produce good crops. And waiting is required. Good farmers and entrepreneurs develop courageous patience.
They know the rhythm of the seasons in their business; they anticipate slow
cycles and adjust accordingly.

Establish patience—courageous patience—as you learn the seasons of your
business. Use experience to help you predict seasons where you will need to
wait and seasons where you will be busy. When is the best time to take a step
back and review? When do you need to hire seasonal help to push you through
a busy time? Become an expert in knowing the pace of your business and go
with it. Think of yourself as a farmer awaiting your crop. With the proper
rains—and time—you will see growth. Don't give up before sowing time.

In what seasons do you need to employ more patience?

Wise men and women are always learning, always listening for fresh insights.

(Proverbs 18:15, MSG)

When you consider timing and patience in growing your business, don't grow weary. Instead pay close attention to the conditions around you and remain flexible. You may discover some golden nugget that can change the course of your journey.

I tell the story in *Soar!* of a fashion designer's journey. This woman longed to be a designer. She worked in women's wear at high-end department stores. She designed beautiful outfits for family and friends. Her clothes were striking and her tailoring was impeccable, yet the timing never worked in her favor for her to launch her label and break out into the land of more than family and friends.

However, the dreamer kept making clothes for those who would pay her while she worked her full-time job. Then, one day, a client noticed a brooch the designer was wearing and inquired about it. The brooch was made of old costume jewelry pieces and discarded fabric from the designer's clothing creations. The client hadn't seen anything like it and wanted to purchase one.

What started off as one sale turned into dozens and hundreds, and eventually the designer realized that there was a market for her uniquely designed brooches. She let go of her desire to create clothes and started thinking of how to profitably make more brooches. The wise woman taught her teenaged daughter and a few of her friends how to make them, and then they branched out to making earrings that matched. Then they started to create necklaces, bracelets, and rings.

A business was born. It may not have been the one the designer originally longed for, but because she paid attention and remained flexible, she was able to launch and sustain a viable and fun business.

How do you remain flexible?

> Who is wise and understanding among you? Let him show by good conduct that
> his works are done in the meekness of wisdom.   (James 3:13, NKJV)

After the devastation of 9/11 in 2001, airlines had to make changes to their policies to keep passengers safe from other terrorist attacks. People could no longer stand in line to use the restroom at the front of the planes. The government restricted certain items in carry-on luggage and several other security measures were put into place.

Now as a result of these stringent rules and regulations that sometimes overlap and infringe on the rights and expectations of customers, some airlines have come under scrutiny because of a handful of situations exposed on social media. Even the airlines are realizing they need to be flexible and adapt to change as they work on customer relations. They are learning from the debacles and adjusting accordingly.

It just goes to show: We all have to adjust. Having a plan that anticipates problems is wise. This example also highlights the importance of incorporating customer feedback in our plans. We used to operate by the mantra "the customer is always right," but wisdom has shown us that this is just not always the case and can be detrimental to a business that caters to customers' every whim, critique, and request without careful evaluation. Yes, customer care is critical to your business and customer satisfaction should be a high priority for all businesses, but business should also have plans to evaluate feedback. The key is to listen but not necessarily act—or act slowly and cautiously.

Businesses are ever changing to address the current conditions. Don't get stuck doing the same old thing if it isn't working. Be wise and understanding.

Are you prepared to adjust to changing conditions?

But solid food is for the mature, who by constant use have trained themselves to
distinguish good from evil.   (Hebrews 5:14, NIV)

Most entrepreneurs are no doubt eager to turn their visions into realities. They are fueled by their passions to create businesses that will soar.
But, again, the wise entrepreneur understands the value of taking baby steps
to avoid the falls and spills that can happen when you run too quickly. There
is a reason most babies begin crawling before walking or drinking milk before
digesting solid foods. It's a process. Respect that process.

Many have learned the importance of taking it slow and testing products
and ideas. For example, even if you decide to outsource products, it is best to
test it before you make a bulk order. No matter how good that discounted price
may be, it is of no value if the product does not meet your standard of quality.
It can actually hurt your business or product to have the item as a part of your
inventory.

You also need to figure out logistical issues such as language barriers or
cultural practices. You can overcome these hurdles easier if you've progressed
lightly and gone slow. The information you gain from testing the waters and the
product will yield results that just can't be matched without the testing. Jumping in feet first is not always the best method.

Going slowly can allow you to make better decisions based on research and
time rather than enthusiasm. Yes, you need to be passionate about your ideas,
but mature people understand the value of proceeding with caution and putting in the work to thoroughly test the ideas before launching fully. Mature
and wise business leaders do not discount the process of learning and growing.
They let the process work—and work through the process.

Where do you need to tread lightly?

Are we all apostles? Are we all prophets? Are we all teachers? Do we all have the power to do miracles? Do we all have the gift of healing? Do we all have the ability to speak in unknown languages? Do we all have the ability to interpret unknown languages? Of course not! (1 Corinthians 12:29-30, NLT)

A lesson most entrepreneurs learn very early in their ventures is to build a team. It is true that no one is an island. We need others to make our businesses soar. Successful leaders are often looking to assemble a talented, unified team to join the flight and help their businesses grow.

It is essential to understand that no matter how talented you are—or how hard you work—you just can't do it all. You can't finance your business, produce as much product as you need, market it, promote it, distribute it, maintain it, and extend your company in new directions—all by yourself. It is not possible. If you try, you will surely crash and burn quickly.

No, a truly smart person realizes that she has certain gifts and skills while different people have just as valuable skills and gifts that are needed in a successful business. So you know when to engage those people with different sets of skills and allow them to function in their areas of expertise. You usually are only as good as your team. If you only rely on yourself, not only will your income be limited but what you can produce will be too. In hands-on businesses, you create a salary cap. You remain limited because you can't duplicate your capabilities or extend your vision.

Learn to prioritize, delegate, pace yourself, and share your vision if increasing the size of your business, influence, and income is important to you. Learn to value the gifts of others and celebrate all you each bring to the table. We are not called to do it all. Utilize the broad spectrum of talent available to you—and watch your business soar.

Who is on your team?

Anyone who meets a testing challenge head-on and manages to stick it out is mighty fortunate. For such persons loyally in love with God, the reward is life and more life.   (James 1:12, MSG)

One of my favorite quotations I use in *Soar!* comes from media mogul Oprah Winfrey. She says: "Failure is another stepping-stone to greatness." I believe Oprah is right, and successful entrepreneurs know this little gem to be true also. Regardless of how carefully you've planned and tested your product or services, stuff will happen. Issues will arise and all problems won't be anticipated or predicted. Unexpected events occur and can send you reeling to the ground if you are not careful. It's important to not let these circumstances and situations keep you on the ground too long. You've got to be ready and willing to bounce back from setbacks quickly.

One way to get back up quickly is to view your failures as stepping stones. Find a way to discharge the painful emotions and look for the lessons. What have you learned from the situation? Did losing that customer help you change your customer service policy to one that has improved your business and attracted new clients? Did selling out of your handmade jewelry cause you to rethink the number of employees you need to meet the demand? Did the bankruptcy from your last venture prompt you to manage finances better for your new business? Each time you fail or fall, there is a clue to your future success. Can you see the stepping stones toward your future?

As I say in *Soar!*, I believe you need to fail boldly if you want to succeed extravagantly. You don't know how many times that successful entrepreneur with the profitable and established business failed. People don't often share the ins and outs of their failures. You may never know their story, but you can rest assured that they have learned to use their failures as steps toward greatness. You can do this, too. Do as the Bible says and meet your challenges head on. Stick out your challenges and use them to propel you to greatness.

What have you learned from failing?

You need to persevere so that when you have done the will of God, you will receive what he has promised.

(Hebrews 10:36, NIV)

Now you may not like the word "failing" or even the thought of viewing setbacks as stepping stones toward your destination. However, if you pick up a tip from many entrepreneurs, you'll learn to enjoy the process of producing your product, and you'll soon realize that part of the process really is trial and error. You can learn so much from just producing. The process becomes your teacher.

Just think about the Wright brothers again. What would have happened if they had lost confidence during the process; surely their idea didn't take flight right away. They went through a process of testing and tinkering; testing again and building upon what they learned worked and what they learned didn't work.

Countless entrepreneurs have done just that: tirelessly tinkered, tweaked, and teased different aspects of their business model until they discovered the perfect blend that worked for their market. Colonel Sanders eventually produced his secret recipe from eleven herbs and spices—after lots of testing. I'm sure his kitchen was filled with recipes that didn't work until he got to what we know as Kentucky Fried Chicken today. And think about how Mark Zuckerberg worked in a dorm room to figure out a way to launch what we now know as Facebook; it didn't start out as the social media machine we now utilize. He went through a process to fine-tune it and make it attractive and usable for the masses.

I agree with Steve Jobs' statement in an entrepreneur.com article. The founder of Apple said, "I'm convinced that about half of what separates the successful entrepreneurs from the non-successful ones is pure perseverance." If you're going to join the ranks of successful business leaders, I suggest you learn to love the process of perfecting your product. It's how you learn to soar.

Do you enjoy the process of producing?

…but a ruler with discernment and knowledge maintains order.

(Proverbs 28:2b, NIV)

Yet another important realization most entrepreneurs discover is that you cannot be everything to everyone. As much as we'd all love to believe everyone desires our products and services, they just don't. And of the biggest mistakes I see entrepreneurs make is casting their customer nets too wide. I think they should go deep rather than wide.

You see, today people have so many choices. There are lots and lots of products and services available-and that makes the entrepreneurial field even more wide open. But you have to know how to make your product unique enough to serve a specific audience. When you've figured out who that is, go after them with all you have.

Focus on where you are and what you have to build upon. Don't get distracted by what your business is not or who doesn't want your product. There's many more fish in the sea and you want to cater your business to catch those fish. You do have to keep your eye on where you are and all that's going on around you with current conditions while at the same time keeping your other eye looking ahead and beyond to your ultimate destination.

Successful entrepreneurs learn to discern quickly. Use customer feedback and information to guide you and help you make the decisions that are best for your customer. Continually study your audience. Predict their trends based on the information at hand—and keep pressing forward. You have a customer base awaiting for your unique brand. Do you and do you well.

How do you stay focused on your customer base?

Those who work their land will have abundant food, but those who chase fantasies will have their fill of poverty.

(Proverbs 28:19, NIV)

Entrepreneurs wear many hats and are aware of the need to keep an eye on the weather conditions at hand. Don't forget about the relational value customers of today are often expecting. You have the opportunity to not only sell a good or service, but you can create relationships which in turn can help you produce a more organic exchange with those you serve.

In fact, at some point you can appear to take the focus off of selling and provide information. And if it is of value to your customers, they will gladly soak it in while patronizing your business and become a brand ambassador. Think about how blogs work. Which ones do you read regularly? (I hope you are following your favorite successful entrepreneurs; you need to hear what they have to say!) Influencers write about issues around them—some may be as simple as what they are doing today, how they handled a certain situation or their thoughts on a current event. All of the time, they are sharing their opinion or perhaps information on a subject that you value. At the end of each blog, you will probably see a tag line advertising their latest project. This is advertising and promotion couched in information sharing. And it is brilliant.

By disseminating free information, these wise entrepreneurs are also sharing their products and establishing their brand. And they are creating an environment where their customers feel valued and connected to them—all while gaining information of interest. It is a win-win situation and one not quickly overlooked by the wise.

How are you creating relational value?

Wisdom cries aloud in the street, in the markets she raises her voice;

at the head of the noisy streets she cries out; at the entrance of the city gates she speaks.

(Proverbs 1:20-21, ESV)

I often try to share constructive criticism with millennial entrepreneurs, many of whom think they should become successful overnight. But there are also some words of wisdom for more seasoned citizens who are either starting businesses or trying to take existing business to another level. Wisdom can be found in multi-generational collaborations.

Many baby boomers have perspectives and views shaped by their experiences and their environment. They grew up thinking that running a successful business required long hours, hard work, self-discipline, and limitless patience. Baby boomers saw parents scrimp, save, and sacrifice and we emulated that fierce work ethic and determination to get ahead at any cost. This hard work effort can be great and beneficial, but it can also produce independent and self-sufficient leaders who are reluctant to ask for help, admit needs, or even accept assistance from willing and capable people. Many people who grew up in the '50s and '60s just think their hard work will get them what they need.

But what older business owners often forsake is the wisdom found in younger people, many of whom grew up with computers, smart phones, and portable electronic devices in their hands. These young people don't even know how to function without technology. They have learned to be efficient with technology while some older entrepreneurs are trying to figure things out the hard way—independent of anyone.

That's why I believe mixing the generations together can be extremely beneficial. Older people can share work ethic and experience while younger leaders can show us how technology can work for us and make our businesses even better. Coming together can save everyone time and energy. It's like wisdom calling out to us; we can do better if we work together.

Do you have a multigenerational team?

> The kings got together, they united and came. (Psalms 48:4, MSG)

The differences in attitudes between generations can be frustrating, but there's plenty to learn from each other if we employ a little understanding and patience.

I definitely believe Millennials have plenty to gain from their parents and grandparents' work ethics. The gutsy grit and tenacity of the Baby Boomer generation can prove beneficial. While hard work isn't the only thing that makes a business successful, you can reap many rewards from it. Many Millennials have come up with a much easier road than their forefathers—and that has been intentional. Many have not had to suffer through lack and have assumed things would be easy. Because of their access to social media and technology, they may underestimate the amount of time and hard work needed to become a success. Didn't this person just blow up on the scene? No one really knows the hard work in the background when all you see is the current glitz and glam tweeted and pictured on Instagram.

All of my biological and most of my spiritually adopted children are a part of the millennial generation, and I often try to help them understand the effort needed to make it in this world. If you are in this generation, avoid allowing a sense of entitlement make you forgo the work. You need to put in the hard work even as you utilize all of the wonderful opportunities now available to you.

And to my baby boomers, don't run from advancement and be open to the new efficient processes made available due to technology. Yes, hard work is still important and critical, yet working smarter is always better. If you are afraid of technology, become a life-long learner and start learning about the new world it has opened up and made available to us. Don't let the new world scare you. Trust me, I frequently need help with downloads, uploads, and every load in between. But I get the help I need and you can too. What a beautiful way to merge the generations than through a mutual exchange of information and help. We're better together.

What do you need to learn from a different generation of leaders?

Your Attitude

Do all things without grumbling or disputing.   (Philippians 2:14, NASB)

I'm convinced that effective leaders have another trait in common: their attitude. Those who succeed often have a constructive attitude. It's more than just being positive. You see, people with a positive attitude hope for the best. They wish and dream about great possibilities and they try to focus on those things. It's great to be positive, but a constructive attitude can be even more beneficial.

People who have constructive attitudes actually make the best of whatever is in front of them so that they can get closer to where they want to be. While these people clearly would like the best to happen, they are not waiting, they are using what they have to get it done. It's the difference between dreaming and doing. With a positive attitude, you dream of the best. With a constructive attitude, you make the best from what you have.

Successful entrepreneurs know that complaining, criticizing, and blame-shifting will not accomplish anything. In fact, all of those attitudes are a waste of time and energy. As the Apostle Paul said in Philippians, it is best to do everything without grumbling or disputing. It gets nothing accomplished and it shifts your mind to negativity. I believe people who constantly complain are not really cut out to be entrepreneurs. You've got to be able to withstand issues and make the most out of situations if you're going to be in business for the long haul.

So the next time you face a challenge, forgo the urge to complain or bemoan what is happening. Instead, focus on what you can do and get it done. This is a far better use of mind space and it sets you up for success.

How's your attitude?

So in everything, do to others what you would have them do to you, for this sums
up the Law and the Prophets   (Matthew 7:12, NIV)

Remember the Golden Rule you learned as a child—to do unto others as you'd like done unto you? It still applies and it can especially be helpful in your business. It's a good exercise to act like your customer and experience your business and industry as a client. When you visit your website, try looking at it as a new viewer. Can you find what you're looking for? How easy is it to order? How does your website look on a smart phone or tablet versus on a computer? (Remember, more and more people surf the net on portable devices these days; your site needs to be helpful for them as well.) Do you accept payment methods your customers use? (Again, there's a whole new generation who has never written a check or even used a credit card—they use apps for payments.)

If you have a physical presence—an office or store—how easy is it to get to your location? How does a potential customer find you? Is parking readily available—and do you have signage to show patrons where to park? What is the first thing a customer feels when he or she walks into your location? Are they greeted warmly or ignored? Do you have what customers need in stock and readily available?

Spend time getting to know exactly what others experience from your business by becoming an "other." Then you will know what needs to be improved. If you don't like something, chances are your customers won't either. Employing the Golden Rule can take your business to another level; it can make you better than your competition. Many people come back to a business because of how they felt during their experience. Make sure your customers feel as you'd like to feel when doing business. Do unto them as you'd like done unto you.

Experience your business as a customer.

Therefore, since we are surrounded by such a great cloud of witnesses, let us throw off everything that hinders and the sin that so easily entangles. And let us run with perseverance the race marked out for us… (Hebrews 12:1, NIV)

Knowing when you are ready for growth requires knowing the conditions around you but also the conditions inside of you. Many people ask me how I knew moving my ministry from West Virginia to Dallas was the right move.

I felt in my gut that there was more to my ministry. It's important to understand that what it takes to build something may not be the same stuff you need to sustain a business. In West Virginia, I had built a ministry from about seven faithful people to more than a thousand. My company had started to produce plays and I had a few bestselling books. For where I was living, I was doing all right. But deep inside, I knew there was more. I knew I was called to do more. I had not maxed out my potential.

I envisioned being able to help the homeless and those in prison and eventually launch an international outreach. Many of my colleagues were not thinking about ancillary ministries; they were bound to more traditional forms. That may have been fine for them, but I was not going to allow myself to be incarcerated by others' perceptions. I needed to follow what I felt God put inside of me. I needed to do what I was called to do…so I stepped out on faith and launched my ministry in a larger, more metropolitan area.

If you, too, feel called to go against the grain and do something different, I must warn you that uniqueness is seldom understood in real time. You will need to pack your faith and listen to what's inside of you to follow your dreams. And here's where mentors can be like your cloud of witnesses (see Hebrews 11 for a list of those whose faith required them to go against the grain). Talk to your mentors about some of the things they experienced as they stepped out on faith; while you will have different stories, you can relate to their inner courage and how they faced critics.

Run the race you've been called to run…and keep the faith.

Time to Grow

> Like newborn babies, crave pure spiritual milk, so that by it you may grow up in
> your salvation…
>
> (1 Peter 2:2, NIV)

Successful leaders understand that growth is necessary to keep their business sustained in flight. What you did to take off is often much different than what you will need to do to keep your business growing. Growth requires dynamic change. Rarely do you want to hire someone just to do a job; you should look for those who want to grow, offer more, and think of ways to improve a process. Even when I hire a gardener for the season, I want him to give me more than he did last year. How has the soil changed? How can we build on the healthy and nourishing conditions he cultivated last year?

It is important that you and your team understand the principle of dynamic change and growth. It can be stifling if someone wants to keep everything the same because they are content and comfortable. That's like leaving the ground and realizing you're still anchored to the hangar. Something is holding you back and your venture will not be able to soar if it is tethered by the timidity of individuals to whom you entrust its maintenance and care.

The role of the leader is to influence all to share the same vision and work toward growth and change. Even if everyone isn't working toward that goal at the same speed, a good leader knows how to inspire the team to see the need to improve and expand the dream and goal. No one sets out to remain at the same level. Even babies drink milk so that they can grow and eat food. A child doesn't start first grade with the intention of staying there for years. And an entrepreneur doesn't invest his or her energy in an endeavor that will stay on the ground or at the same level.

You were meant to soar—and you'll only get there by growing.

What are you doing to grow your business?

"Well done, my good servant!" his master replied. "Because you have been trustworthy in a very small matter, take charge of ten cities."   (Luke 19:17, NIV)

To measure the success of your business, you have to know your metrics. You have to know why you are in business and how to measure your impact. Is it through profit, purpose, or power? Usually it is a combination of all three.

You need to know the level of results your efforts have on your department, company, community, city, and society. Metrics are like a stopwatch for a runner. They are used to track success. You don't just think a business is successful because it has existed for a long time; you look at its profits. And if you're running a nonprofit, you look at your purpose. Were you able to accomplish it? How much did it cost to reach your goal? Were you on budget, etc.?

You cannot ignore the metrics if you are striving for success. It's another way of determining how you are investing in your business. Wise leaders follow the example of the good servant in the parable in Luke 19. They are good stewards over what they have. They look for ways to make sure they are meeting their profits, purpose, and utilizing their power to grow their business. That's how they measure success.

Make sure your eye is on your metrics. Know what makes you a success and track it often. Don't lose sight of what makes you impactful. You don't want to waste your time and energy when you are not meeting your metrics. You need to know the difference between what's working *for* you and what's working *on* you!

What metrics guide you?

"'Yes,' the king replied, 'and to those who use well what they are given, even more will be given. But from those who do nothing, even what little they have will be taken away…'"

(Luke 19:26, NLT)

We all have a lot to learn from the parable of the talents Jesus tells in Luke 19 (and Matthew 25). I love this parable because it shows how God honors our faithfulness. We are all given different amounts of talents and skills—and what matters most is what we each do with those skills. It's not a competition. You're not expected to be someone you are not. Instead, you are expected to do the best you can with what you have been given. Invest your gifts and skills well and see the return on your investment.

However, there is a strong warning for those who do not invest their talents. They are like the third servant in the parable. Instead of taking the one talent, or money, he had and investing it, he did nothing. He hid it because he was afraid of the master. He didn't want to lose the money. Yet, he made no initiative to use what he had to make more. His master called him lazy and took the little talent away from him.

Don't be like the third servant, hiding your gifts thinking you'd do more if you had more. No, look at what God has given you and only you. Think of ways to use exactly what you have. Don't allow fear to keep you grounded. And don't become lazy or compare what you have to anyone else. God has planted seeds inside each and every one of us in different measures. Be faithful and water the seeds you have to produce fruit. You will be given more when you invest what you already have.

How are you investing your talents (gifts and skills)?

Plans fail for lack of counsel, but with many advisers they succeed.

(Proverbs 15:22, NIV)

Every airline at each airport has a crew of people who perform jobs on the ground that will help the plane soar. Likewise, successful entrepreneurs also have a solid ground crew in place to help their businesses fly. Ideally, they have three kinds of crewmembers: supporters, advisers, and mentors. These relationships—each serving different functions—can lay the groundwork for the smooth runway needed to take flight.

Your supporters, often family members, serve as your cheerleaders. They are the ones who celebrate your successes and help you gain perspective when things fail. They are your sounding boards. They can also provide practical help, such as picking up the kids from school, cooking meals, or helping with other chores you may have to neglect when running your business. Your supporters care deeply about you and want to see you succeed. They understand the stress running a business can give you and they want to help lift that load where they can. They provide personal, emotional support through this grueling process.

Your advisers are usually counselors who provide professional and intellectual support. Your advisers may also care about you personally, but first and foremost, they want to see you employ the best business practices. They may be in business themselves and have wisdom to share from their own experiences.

Your mentors are often a combination of supporters and advisers. They may offer comprehensive insight into how to juggle your life's demands as you make your business soar. Your mentors want you to succeed both professionally and personally—and they are looking out for you in both areas. They have experience and are willing to guide you toward success.

Don't underestimate the value of your ground crew and don't be afraid to lean on them. They are your support system.

Who is on your ground crew?

A gift opens doors; it gives access to the great.   (Proverbs 18:16, NRSV)

In addition to your supportive ground crew, you need a flight crew to help you soar. Your flight crew often is those who can help fund your venture. They offer more than emotional support or personal encouragement; they offer capital.

You must be your first investor. You have to be willing to invest your own financial resources into your business. How can you expect anyone else to believe in your business if you haven't looked carefully at your resources and allocated some for your dream?

Of course, deciding how much to invest in your own business can be tricky. Think about the amount you can afford to lose in your investment—or the amount you will not need until you can earn it back (after you've paid your expenses). If you can't afford to lose any money right now, you may need to wait until you can save enough to properly stake your business. Unfortunately, many beginning entrepreneurs deplete their savings, retirement fund, and equity in their homes to get their business off the ground. They are driven by their enthusiasm and adrenaline, but it takes more than that to successfully run a business.

When you know how much you can invest, you know how much more you will need from outside investors. Look to business leaders who have successful operations already. They understand what is needed and are often willing to help those following their path. If they turn you down, respectfully ask them to share their reasons for not investing. You can learn valuable information from their feedback, which can help you with your next pitch to another potential investor.

Then, when you have investors, make sure you get your agreement in writing. Spell out the amount they will invest as well as the amount you will return and at which point in the venture you will return the money (usually once you have a certain amount of profit). An attorney or accountant can help you here. And also make sure you are clear on what role your investors will play beyond providing financial support, if any. Know the difference between an investor who is risking capital and a partner, director, or stakeholder.

Who is on your flight crew?

One who has unreliable friends soon comes to ruin, but there is a friend who
sticks closer than a brother.   (Proverbs 18:24, NIV)

Many new entrepreneurs find themselves needing to look to family and friends to become a part of their flight crew. They need capital from those closest to them. While it may seem like family and friends would be more likely to support you, it is not always the case. And when family and friends do agree to join your flight team, you need to make sure your boundaries and expectations are clear. Discuss the specifics with your family members or friends just as you would with any other investor. Then write everything down, including what happens if the business fails and they lose their investment.

You may ask them how they would feel if they lost their investment, and you should consider how this might impact the dynamics of your relationship. You need to discuss this *before* you're stuck at Thanksgiving dinner and no one will pass the turkey to you!

Your contract is critical. Don't worry about feeling uncomfortable asking for their signature on a contract. You have asked for the money—and they have agreed to support you—so give them the courtesy you would any other investor. It could save your relationship.

And just as you would with other investors, make sure you outline your family member's or friend's role in the business. Will they have access to your operations, practices and records? Will they have a say in what happens? Gathering capital for your business puts you one step closer to launching. And if you have the financial support from those close to you, be grateful. But be wise as well. Loyal relationships can be hard to come by. Don't let your business get in the way of a dear relationship.

Have family members or close friends joined your flight crew?

Clearly, you are a letter from Christ showing the result of our ministry among you. This "letter" is written not with pen and ink, but with the Spirit of the living God. It is carved not on tablets of stone, but on human hearts.

(2 Corinthians 3:3, NLT)

Sometimes Christians think they need to sell a certain product or be in a certain type of business to be profitable for God's kingdom. This is just not true. We need to occupy the world with businesses that are needed. And when we are doing business, we can be lights for God's kingdom.

It's just like the scripture says: Our lives are often letters for others. People may not read the Bible but they know how you treat them. They observe your business practices and services and can be drawn to God through your actions. You don't have to evangelize through words all of the time; your actions show loud and clear. They can be like a letter to a person, showing the love and character of God.

You have a great opportunity to show others the character of God through your business dealings. You represent God by the way you operate, and how you treat your customers and your employees. Use what God has given you to be a letter to someone else. Be faithful in the small things and remain diligent. Keep your principles and faith and watch as others are drawn to you and the God in you.

Your business doesn't have to say Christian or sell crosses or Bibles to be a company governed by Christian principles. You may be able to attract more people by being faithful and Christ-like in your daily operations. It's a great way to honor God as you use your gifts and skills.

Do you think your business represents God well to others?

Define Yourself

Words kill, words give life; they're either poison or fruit—you choose.

(Proverbs 18:21, MSG)

Knowing when to leave your launching pad and begin your business or expand it is critical. But even more important is knowing that you and only you must define yourself. When you move according to your own definition of success, you know your goals, not someone else's. I'm not saying you will not adjust and adapt—because you should. But you need to be who you want to be and know where you want to go.

Imagine if I had listened to others and allowed them to define me. I would not have had the confidence to leave West Virginia to continue to build my ministry in Dallas. I would have allowed other people's questions to make me doubt my vision and myself. I would have been wondering about my own goals and asking myself: Why leave a place that is comfortable? I would have thought that the level of success I had was enough. I would have allowed the words of others to kill my dreams.

But thankfully, I didn't allow those questions to enter my mind and cause me to doubt myself. I didn't listen to their "deadly" words; instead, I followed the words that I knew would give me life and help me to bring into existence what I saw in my mind and heart.

To be successful, you have to guard against the negative words people say and the negative thoughts others will try to put into your mind. It is easy to stay in the same place and continue to do the same thing. It takes courage, faith, and confidence to move forward and break the mold. And it takes knowing who you are and your purpose in life. Don't listen to the voices from others; follow your own inner compass. Follow where you believe God leads you. Then and only then will you know what success looks like for you.

Whose voice are you listening to?

Pride first, then the crash, but humility is precursor to honor.

(Proverbs 18:12, MSG)

If you find your business stalled, one of the things that may be keeping it from soaring is your desire to do everything. Many times employing professionals to handle certain aspects of your business is more efficient than trying to do everything yourself. I know you want to have a hand in all parts of creating your baby, but sometimes it is best to outsource certain tasks and let a professional handle it.

You may be able to handle your books with great software and what you learned in your economics class in college, but a professional accountant who only works with money knows much more than you do and can often offer services that will make you operate better. And you'll be amazed at how much more energy you have just by relinquishing some duties. You may think it only takes up one hour of your day or week to manage your books, but you'll find that using two or three hours of energy instead to employ a professional can greatly reduce stress.

Unless finance is your thing, you may find that you don't have the time or patience to learn all of the ins and outs that will benefit your business. You can consider hiring a bookkeeper, tax attorney, or certified public accountant (CPA). Many of these professionals will have experience dealing with entrepreneurs who own their own businesses like you do. They can lead you in the right direction and save you time—time you can devote to taking your business to the next level by investing in your areas of expertise.

Don't get caught thinking you have to save money by doing everything yourself. Sometimes your time is worth more than the dollars you will save and the newly discovered creative energy can yield much more. Getting professional help is often the catalyst for new growth.

What can you outsource to a professional?

Watch Your Money

God cares about honesty in the workplace; your business is his business.

(Proverbs 16:11, MSG)

While I advocate outsourcing some of your business functions, like book-keeping and accounting, if that is not your forte, I also remind entrepreneurs to always sign their own checks. It's vital to know where your money is going, and having control over who gets paid keeps your eyes on your money. If you can't sign each check, set up your accounts where two signatures are required. This way you have a system of checks and balances, so to speak, and one person can't write checks without someone else knowing.

Unfortunately, you have to be on the lookout for issues such as embezzlement and theft. The most honest person can be tempted to "take a little off the top" when they think no one else is looking. And not all financial losses are related to dishonesty. But if you are signing each check, you will better be able to notice inconsistencies quickly. You can notice if cost of goods are rising and perhaps shift your price point or negotiate with vendors to get another product or price. You wouldn't know to look into the matter if you weren't signing checks or reviewing your costs regularly.

By doing so, you send a message to your employees working for you. You let them know that while they are a valuable part of the team, you are still the one in charge and handling the money. You are minding your business—and the business they have signed up to help grow. Even if you feel you do not have the time or that you do not enjoy it, you still have your eyes on the bottom line. You can instill confidence in your workers just by being a good steward and keeping your eye on what's important.

Sign your own checks.

Then he ordered the crowds to sit down on the grass, and taking the five loaves and the two fish, he looked up to heaven and said a blessing. Then he broke the loaves and gave them to the disciples, and the disciples gave them to the crowds. And they all ate and were satisfied. And they took up twelve baskets full of the broken pieces left over. And those who ate were about five thousand men, besides women and children.

(Matthew 14:19-21, ESV)

Many entrepreneurs do not like marketing. They see it as just something they have to do like filing taxes. But marketing can be the engine that drives your business to soar.

One way to help market your business or brand is to use your mission. If you can incorporate it into your marketing, it becomes much more organic and you might get excited. Early in my career, I realized that everything I did had a common element. From my ministry to music to movies and more, I had a desire to inform, inspire, and entertain. I was all about transforming lives through these three pillars. As I built my brand and considered next projects, I made sure they were connected to informing, inspiring and/or entertaining. Each book I chose to write, each ministry event I planned, each movie I produced fell under one of those areas.

When it came time to market each project, I already knew my mission and used it in the marketing. And my brand becomes even clearer as my team and I build marketing around any project. Think of how Jesus' mission helped to market him. This is not heretical; just think about marketing as spreading the word about what Jesus was doing and all He had to offer. I bet the miracle of Jesus feeding 5,000 with only five loaves of bread and two fish spread like wildfire. Witnesses to the miracle told everyone they knew and then those people told even more people.

By simply (or not so simply) doing what He came to do—His mission— Jesus marketed the good news about himself. Likewise, think of ways you can organically show more and more people exactly what you do and why you do it. That's marketing—and it can change the trajectory of your business.

How are you marketing your mission?

You are the light of the world. A town built on a hill cannot be hidden.

(Matthew 5:14, NIV)

In *Soar!,* I mention the importance of marketing several times. I do this intentionally because I think many Christians have trouble tooting their own horns. We've been told to be modest and not to brag, but when it comes to business, you have to get the word out.

What good is it to write a great book that can transform many lives if no one even knows the book exists? You have to share the book with others to get them to read it. You have to make some of the content known to encourage them to download the entire package. And, quite frankly, most readers need to know something about the author to want to pick up a book and read his or her words. It's not bragging, it is promoting your mission and message.

Likewise, how can you grow your real estate business if potential customers have no idea where to find you? Or create a successful catering service if hungry event planners do not know you are out there? No matter what great service you have to offer, if no one knows about it, it really doesn't matter. It won't sell unless it is promoted. Somehow, some way, your intended audience has to find you—and that means you have to find them and let them know about your business.

Promotions can be fun if you put a little creative thinking behind it. Think about whom you want to reach and where they are—then go after that audience. When we were promoting *Jumping the Broom,* I knew my target audience was African American women. I also knew that this demographic frequented beauty shops and often received valuable information from their beauticians. So, we made aprons for stylists and beauticians with the movie's title and gave them as gifts at an early screening. When people showed up for their hair appointment, they learned about this movie. That got them talking and looking forward to seeing it. Mission accomplished! Our targeted audience saw the light!

How do you think about promotions?

No one lights a lamp and then puts it under a basket. Instead, a lamp is placed on a
stand, where it gives light to everyone in the house.   (Matthew 5:15, NLT)

Creating and sustaining your business takes more than talent and skill.
Your marketing plan and strategy is just as important, if not more important, than your product or service. Why? Because what good is an ingenious
product or excellent service if no one knows about it?

It's like what Jesus said to His followers about their good work; they were
not to hide their work but to show it to the world. Not for vain glory, but so
others could come to know Christ and this new way of life. Our promotions are
not based on showing ourselves off to the world; they're based on sharing the
service or product we have been blessed to create, assigned to be a good steward
over. And how else will people know about all you have to offer, if you don't
light that candle and put it high on a stand for it to shine brightly?

Today, promoting and marketing can be easier than ever. You have social
media on every smartphone; you can use these platforms to share information
about your business. And you can get others actively involved in sharing your
message—it's as simple as a retweet or a quick selfie with your product. Running a business can be exciting to some, producing the products and services
they've worked so hard to bring to light. But the wise one doesn't skip the marketing and promotion strategies. While they may not be your passion—sharing
your business is—promotions provide the avenue to get the word out.

What's your promotion strategy?

"And no one puts new wine into old wineskins. For the old skins would burst
from the pressure, spilling the wine and ruining the skins. New wine is stored in
new wineskins so that both are preserved."   (Matthew 9:16, NLT)

Another tip I offer entrepreneurs who are looking to take their business to
another level and soar higher is to revisit your basic marketing messages.
What worked last year or the year before, may not even be applicable any more.
What got you off the ground may not be what keeps you in the air. You may
need to refresh your messaging to make it more applicable to who you and your
business have become.

Your marketing should reflect your brand—and that can change after take-
off. Ask yourself if your message is still aligned with your mission. It's a good
idea to sit down and think about the following questions—with your team or
alone—periodically. What is it you specifically want to convey to your market
about your business or services? What is the story you want to share? What is
it that you want others to know about you and your company? What values do
you want to communicate to your customers?

Also think about your customers and where to find them. Are you sending
your messages to places they still frequent? Is there a new way you can engage
potential customers? Are they frequenting another platform? Do they congre-
gate in a certain place? And, are you and your message in the same places as your
potential customers? Answering these questions can help you decide if your
marketing is still on point or whether it needs tweaking or a complete overall.
Having marketing checkups can keep your business healthy and inspire growth.

Have you checked your messaging lately?

Then the man said, "Your name will no longer be Jacob, but Israel, because you have struggled with God and with humans and have overcome."

(Genesis 32:28, NIV)

Have you ever paid attention to some of the Biblical stories where people receive a new name after a life-altering event? Jacob, once a trickster, became known as Israel, the father of the sons who make up the twelve tribes of the Jewish nation. Saul became Paul when he went from being a prosecutor of Christians to a witness for Christ who wrote much of the New Testament (see Acts 13:9); Abram and his wife Sarai became Abraham and Sarah (see Genesis 17:5,15).

It's almost as if after their life-altering experiences, their old names just didn't do them justice. Names describe us and so does the name of your business. And just like people, sometimes we outgrow our names or need to alter them to fit our new persona or brand. Don't feel like you have to stick with the name you originally began with. If it doesn't work, change it. If it is too long and has become more known for its initials, then use those. You can brainstorm new ideas that will better connect with your audience. Having the right name for your business is important and shouldn't be taken lightly. Your name represents your business. Its impact should be reflected in its name.

In *Soar!*, I tell a story about a spa owner who had a rather clever and meaningful name for her business. She named it Lapastii Ater Soror, which means beautiful black sister. Sure, the meaning of the name connects with her target audience and what she offered, but who could pronounce that name? And how many people realized she offered beauty treatments? While she could argue that people would be intrigued and ask her the meaning, I wouldn't bet on it. Do you think people were even able to spell that name well enough to search for it on Google? The name didn't communicate specifically what she did or offered nor did it present any kind of emotional message. The wise entrepreneur did eventually change her spa's name. She realized that her messaging begins with the name of her business—and so does yours.

Is your business name working for you?

Pleasant words are like a honeycomb, sweet and delightful to the soul and healing to the body.

                                                     (Proverbs 16:24, AMP)

Now that you have ensured that your name delivers the right message about your business and stands out from your competition, it is time to think about your logo. Your company's name and logo are a central part of everything you do; they should be prominent on your business cards, storefront designs, interior décor, website, social media, advertising, and promotional materials.

Your logo can also simply be the font you use to display your name—but it should be consistent every time it is seen. That includes keeping the same color scheme. At some point, a customer should recognize your business simply from the logo or your colors. Think of the bulls-eye for Target; you don't need to see the brand name spelled out when you see the red and white circle. You also know clearly what brand is being promoted when you see golden arches. The McDonald's logo is as much a part of its brand as the actual name.

You can also use your logo and name in creative ways to deliver your company's messages. Often times it takes time for your name and logo to stick in the public's mind—another reason to make sure it is consistent. You are creating memories in customers' and potential customers' minds through what you show them.

You should employ the same strategy for any slogans you may use in marketing material. People should hear and see your name, logo, and slogan together, signaling your mission. Think of some of the slogans that have stuck over time. I bet you know them: "You're in good hands" (Allstate Insurance); "Have it your way" (Burger King); and "Just do it" (Nike). Use your name, logo and slogans to convey memorable and positive messages about your businesses—and your customers will not forget your business!

Evaluate your name, logo, and slogan.

The mouth of a good person is a deep, life-giving well...   (Proverbs 10:11, NIV)

According to marketing guru Seth Godin, "Marketing is no longer about the stuff that you make, but about the stories you tell." Haven't you noticed how commercials now seem like mini-movies? People respond to stories much more than over-the-top, in-their-face promotions.

What story are you sharing with your marketing and messaging? Is it the best narrative to bring in a new customer or to sustain the business? What roles does your customer play in the story? How can you engage them actively? Think about what you want people to experience from your business. What do you want them to feel after using your product or service? What need do you want to spark inside of them so that they will make a purchase? Focus on the problem that you are solving for your customer. You could be making life more convenient or efficient for them; perhaps you are delivering quality, reliability or some combination of all of these desires.

Pay attention to messages that attract you. What have people gotten into? Remember when everyone was posting videos in the Ice Bucket Challenge? These videos went viral and each one mentioned the ALS Association, who started the challenge in hopes of getting people to make donations to their organization and become aware of its mission. The association spent nothing as celebrities, kids and the average person marketed a story for them.

Or look at how the Susan G. Komen Foundation has utilized the color pink to brand their Breast Cancer Awareness mission. They have football players wearing pink in October. When I was little, businesses often sponsored kids' sports teams. All it took was creating T-shirts (hopefully in your business colors) with your company's name plastered on the front or back. Each time that team played, dozens of kids (and their consumer parents) showed up as walking billboards for designated businesses.

Be creative when you think about sharing your story; it can make marketing more fun and much more meaningful.

What story do you want to tell?

More on Marketing

Unfriendly people care only about themselves; they lash out at common sense.

(Proverbs 18:1, NLT)

As you may have noticed, I'm big on marketing. It's an important step for any successful venture. People have got to know about your great service and product. I encourage you to think of ways to align yourself with other companies who may sell something different than you do but have a similar audience. What can you offer to help that business or organization and at the same time, share your story with their audience?

Think of causes that are naturally or logically related to your business. For example, a baby boutique might want to sponsor a local marathon that promotes weight loss and wellness for moms. Or how about writing a blog post for mothers on a popular mommy blog? If you run a car repair business, perhaps you could partner with Uber, Lyft, or another car service to offer free transportation on certain nights or offer a discount to people who are having their cars repaired at the time. You could also volunteer to speak to a local group and provide tips for small business owners and entrepreneurs.

You can also consider donating a certain amount of your products as part of the swag bags at certain cause-driven events that will attract your audience. Or offer discounts specially designed to get people to sample your products or services. Give a prize in a raffle for a charitable organization. Your name and your product will be printed up on each of those raffle tickets, and while there is only one winner, there could be a large number of people reading your company's name. Not to mention the number of times someone shares what the prizes are as they try to get someone to purchase a ticket—it's an economical way to get your name in front of others and it benefits charity.

Smart business owners know that marketing is critical and it isn't enough to simply be good and offer the best service. If you get behind a cause, it can ignite a viral wildfire and increase your sales exponentially.

Who can you partner with to market your business?

> When the queen of Sheba heard about the fame of Solomon and his relationship
> to the Lord, she came to test Solomon with hard questions.　(1 Kings 10:1, NIV)

Success is not just what you know—it's also about who you know! Even the Queen of Sheba, who had a level of success herself, increased her network and her net worth when she reached out to King Solomon. She reached out to meet this man. Successful entrepreneurs know the value of expanding their network with strategic relationships.

Having the best product and producing the best service can go a long way, but you need to get the word out—and one way to do that is to use your network! When I say use, I don't mean in an abusive or negative way. What I am suggesting is that you consider the people in your network and utilize those connections to expose your business to a wider audience.

Some creative marketing is all about relationships. You may own a t-shirt design company. How much exposure do you think you'd get if a popular rapper wore your shirt at an event—one where the artist would be captured in lots of photos and videos that would be tweeted and retweeted millions of times? But, you don't know the artist. How will you get your shirt to him or her? You may have someone in your network who is friends with a friend of the artist's stage manager or publicist. Shooting a quick email or text to request a mailing address is really all you need—or you can show up at a concert with the shirt in hand and give it to the right person to deliver it. You've just used your network to get more exposure than a paid ad could ever hope to yield.

Some people in your network may be connectors—putting you in contact with a whole new world; others can be what Malcolm Gladwell calls mavens. These people know lots of information. They know what's on sale everywhere; they know all about different products and functions. They enjoy finding out this information and sharing it with others. By all means, use mavens to help get the word out about your business.

Who are your connectors? Your mavens?

The Value of Preparation

We can make our own plans, but the Lord gives the right answer...

Commit your actions to the Lord, and your plans will succeed.

(Proverbs 16:1–3, NLT)

My family and friends often tease me because of my style of preaching. They know I like to build my sermons around fresh interpretations of Scripture while using surprising metaphors or unexpected examples. Others compliment me on both my content and style of delivery. They say I have a natural and effortless way of presenting Biblical truths. While I'm honored by their compliments and I give God the glory for inspiring my messages, people would be amazed at the amount of preparation that goes into planning my sermons.

I prepare, read, research, pray, and organize my thoughts each time I speak. I do this because I'm convinced that preparation facilitates liberation. I can be free to improvise and make my messages fit the context of my specific audience because of the hard work I've done in preparation. The better I know my text, the better I'm able to go off script and deliver a point that will fly. It's the preparation and support beneath the surface that allows me to be comfortable enough to improvise.

Preparation and flexibility go hand in hand. I need to have my main points in mind—my destination, where I want to take my audience—and how I'm going to get us there—my transportation, the examples and ideas supporting my main point. Delivering these sermons is similar to launching a business. Plenty of preparation is needed as you plan to get from point A to B. And the more prepared you are, the better you're able to take advantage of any opportunities that might crop up along the way.

How prepared are you for your next leg of the journey?

Customer Service

Hope deferred makes the heart sick, but a dream fulfilled is a tree of life.

(Proverbs 13:12, NLT)

Let's get real: no one starts a business with the intention of failing. Everyone who launches a venture wants to succeed. Naturally, success should be defined by your own terms. Some people want to make a lot of money, others want to have a sustainable business to pass on to their children or others, while still others want the flexibility of creating their own hours and being their own boss.

Today's scripture reminds us that "hope deferred makes the heart sick, but a longing fulfilled is a tree of life." You don't want to plant something and watch it wither and die; you want to see your dream fulfilled like a tree bursting forth with abundant leaves and sweet fruit. You want a strong, sturdy tree of life.

To get there—regardless of how you define success—how you treat your customer will be important. Placing your customers' needs high on your priority list is one way to achieve this goal. While your marketing and promotions, and of course the product you provide, is important, your business will flourish if people have a quality experience. Don't spend all of your time and energy focusing only on your product. Remember to keep your customer in mind so you can get to success—however you may define it. You want your dream to be fulfilled.

Rate your customer service.

Abel also brought a gift—the best portions of the firstborn lambs from his flock.
The Lord accepted Abel and his gift…   (Genesis 4:4, NLT)

In *Soar!*, I mention several Biblical characters who can serve as wonderful role models in our entrepreneurial quests. They may have lived long before entrepreneur was a known word, but their character and actions are still applicable for today's business leader. Many are listed in the hall of fame, or cloud of witnesses, in Hebrews 11. I'd like to lift up some of their examples in the next few entries.

You may know the story of brothers Cain and Abel. Cain worked in the field while Abel was a shepherd. When it was time to make an offering to God, Abel gave his best first-born lamb. Cain gave some crops (see Genesis 4). Scripture says that God accepted Abel's offering but He did not accept Cain's. Those familiar with the story know Cain goes on to kill his brother. When he is confronted, we get the famous quote, "Am I my brother's keeper?" God then punishes Cain.

But Abel shows us something important here. He gives his best. This is the epitome of an entrepreneur. We should strive to always give our best—our best ideas, our best energy, our best work to our business, which serves as an act of honoring God, the giver of our gifts and skills. The Bible doesn't say specifically why God didn't accept Cain's offering, but it is assumed that Cain's offering was not his best, it was just "some of his crops." It could have been his leftovers, or perhaps he gave little thought to what he was offering. He didn't do as Abel did and present his very best.

Our best represents God. It's as if we are working unto Him (see Colossians 3:23), and it shows we care to work and develop what God has instilled in us.

Are you giving your best?

Adam had relations with his wife again, and she had another son and called his name Seth, for she said, "God has granted me another offspring instead of Abel because Cain killed him."

(Genesis 4:25, MEV)

The story of Adam and Eve's third child is not as well known as the story of Cain and Abel, but the story of Seth does still provide inspiration to those faithful enough to follow their entrepreneurial dreams. After Cain killed Abel, God punished him. His crops did not produce well or without lots of trouble, and Abel became a "wanderer" (Genesis 4:12). But God did give him protection.

But Adam and Eve lost both of their sons—one to a senseless murder and the other was a fugitive because of his actions. However, Seth shows what happens when you don't give up. Scripture says Adam and Eve kept on living and even had "relations." They didn't let their predicament of being exiled from the Garden or mourning from the loss of their sons stop them from living. They came together and were still fruitful. And they were given another son.

When you feel lost, exiled, or even punished, I implore you to remember the gift of Seth. It's never too late to birth a new child who can carry forward your legacy. This entrepreneurial lifestyle is not always easy. Disappointment will come; there will be times when you feel like giving up, and in some instances, there will be times when you do lose business. But keep on living, keep on listening to the fire inside of you—and birth another baby. Don't give up—your Seth may be right around the corner. (And Seth lived for 912 years—see Genesis 5:8!)

How does Seth's story inspire you?

By faith Noah, when warned about things not yet seen, in holy fear built an ark
to save his family. By his faith he condemned the world and became heir of the
righteousness that is in keeping with faith.   (Hebrews 11:7, NIV)

The story of Noah is probably much more familiar, but it is always great
to review it and find new inspiration. Noah was known as a righteous
man (Genesis 6:9). He lived amongst others who were not righteous and God
decided to flood the land. However, God wanted to save Noah and his family so
He told him to build an ark. But it wasn't yet raining. Noah could have chosen
to doubt and not follow God's instructions, but he didn't. Noah chose to be
faithful and do exactly what God commanded.

Noah picked up a hammer and started to build something that probably
made no sense to anyone else. He followed God's lead and it not only saved his
life, but his family's as well as the human race. Taking steps forward can be
our biggest challenge as entrepreneurs. And this is where faith steps in. Don't
leave your faith out of your business. When you've done the planning and the
research and the testing, make sure you remember to include your faith. This
is where you learn to trust God even more. You know that hard work and planning can yield great results, but you also rely on God to do what you cannot do.
Even when things look bleak, follow God. Trust God and watch how you soar!

How can you find inspiration from Noah?

But Ruth replied, "Don't ask me to leave you and turn back. Wherever you go, I will go; wherever you live, I will live. Your people will be my people, and your God will be my God. Wherever you die, I will die, and there I will be buried. May the Lord punish me severely if I allow anything but death to separate us!"

(Ruth 1:16, NLT)

One thing you need for sure if you're going to be an entrepreneur is the courage to take risks.

Ruth was a risk taker. Her full story is found in the book bearing her name. As mentioned earlier, there are only four short chapters so if you are not familiar with her story, treat yourself and read about her life. I'll summarize her story to point out the risks she took. Ruth was married to one of Naomi's sons. They lived in Moab, but Naomi and her family were originally from Bethlehem. They left when there was a famine in the land. After a while, the men in Naomi's family—her husband and two sons—died. Naomi was left alone in the foreign land of Moab with her two daughters-in-law, Ruth and Orpah.

Now you might think that doesn't sound like she is alone, but Naomi *felt* alone. When her daughters-in-law wanted to follow her back to her hometown of Bethlehem, she told them to stay in Moab. Ruth, however, refused. She risked leaving the land she knew, the land where her family still lived, to be a companion to her mother-in-law. Ruth accompanied Naomi all the way back to Bethlehem. Her risks don't stop there. While in Bethlehem, Ruth decided to take on dangerous work in the fields to provide for Naomi and herself. There, she garnered the attention of the wealthy land owner. The care she provided for her mother-in-law was duly noted and Ruth became desirable to the man, Boaz.

One of Ruth's rewards for the big risks she took was a marriage to Boaz. They also had a child, who was a forefather of the great King David and later, Jesus Himself. Talk about a reward for taking a risk. When you step out on faith, you don't know exactly how you will be rewarded—but Ruth shows us that faithfulness is worth the risk.

Are you willing to take a risk?

It was by faith that Rahab the prostitute was not destroyed with the people in her city who refused to obey God. For she had given a friendly welcome to the spies.

(Hebrews 11:31, NLT)

Another risk taker from the Bible is Rahab. Her story also reminds us of the rewards available to those who are willing to take a risk. Rahab lived in Jericho during the time the Israelites were scouting out the land. God had told them that they would receive this Promised Land and they were checking it out before conquering. The Israelite spies ran across Rahab, who hid them in her house.

Rahab had heard about the God of Israel and all He was capable of doing. She had faith in God and knew the Israelites would soon take over the land. She activated her faith by helping the Israelite spies. When her countrymen came looking for the spies, Rahab refused to give them up. She denied that they were in her home and sent her men looking for them elsewhere.

To keep the Israelite spies safe, Rahab was smart enough to make a deal with them. Because she had confidence in their God and knew they would soon conquer Jericho, she asked that they kept her and her family safe during the invasion. The spies agreed—as long as Rahab kept her end of the bargain. This woman's quick thinking, knowledge of the God of Israel, and trust in God not only kept her safe but it also saved the lives of her family. Her risks were rewarded.

Do you believe your risks will be rewarded?

I will instruct you and teach you in the way you should go; I will counsel you with
my loving eye on you.   (Psalm 32:8, NIV)

As business owners and entrepreneurs, I think it is important not to lose
sight of sharing with others. I think we need to participate in the exchange
of knowledge with an investment in people, particularly young ones who may
look to us for guidance.

It's a type of paying it forward when you share information with a young person. You are building a bridge from the present to the future. This can build your
business—as you will no doubt learn from the exchange, too—but it will also
build our communities and future generations. The relationships we develop
when we exchange information can look much like the Psalm in today's scripture. It says that God has a loving eye on us. That in and of itself can bring solace
to you—knowing that God has you in his view. We should follow this example
and keep our eye on those looking to follow in our footsteps as well as others.

By teaching what you know to another person, you can build their confidence
and help them find their purpose in life. By sharing with your peers, you can
often find solutions and empathic ears. Your peers understand what you're going
through. And by sharing with those who may be older than you or have more experience in business, you can gain knowledge and wisdom to continue the cycle of
giving to others. Remember to teach someone else, reach out to your peers, and
glean from those who are succeeding. It can be a beautiful cycle of give and take.

Participate in the cycle of exchanging information.

> Good planning and hard work lead to prosperity, but hasty shortcuts lead to
> poverty.
> (Proverbs 21:5, NLT)

While finances may not be your thing, I cannot emphasize enough or overstate its importance. Do not run away from the financial planning component of your business nor bury your hand in the sand. To be successful, you need to make sound financial decisions and this includes good planning.

You may need to utilize consultants to help you in this area. Don't be afraid to reach out to good accountants, lawyers, lenders, and investors. When you start your business, you need to know clearly where your capital will come from. Create an income statement and project how you will establish profitability. Be sure to create a realistic prediction about income so you will know when to expect to see a profit. And know what you will do in the mean time until you can claim a profit. Where will the money come from?

Cash flow is often overlooked but it can be one of the biggest problems for new businesses. You may be expecting income, but it may not come at the time and rate you expect it to. In order to keep functioning, you will need cash to flow, usually from other sources. You also need to consider if your profits will be seasonal, and if so, how will you make up for the low periods? Make sure you identify the low and high seasons; just as you need to know where your money will come from in low seasons, you need to make sure you do not overspend during the times of high profitability. Be on the lookout for special occurrences where you may have gotten a larger influx of business. Don't mistake these times for trends; that could erroneously change your budget or spending habits, which could backfire on you.

Regardless of your opinion on finances, make sure you handle your business when operating your venture. It is critical.

**How do your financial plans for business look? How often do you
review them?**

Cast your cares on the Lord and he will sustain you; he will never let the righteous be shaken. (Psalm 55:22, NIV)

In *Soar!*, I talk about the historic demise of the Silver Bridge that stretched along the Ohio River. In 1967, when I was a child, this bridge collapsed right at rush hour. In less than a minute, more than thirty vehicles fell into the cold river, killing forty-six people who were crossing the bridge at the time. The engineers who inspected the ruins of the structure concluded that the bridge had been supporting more weight than intended. When the bridge was first built, vehicles were a lot lighter. Over time, automobiles were heavier and larger. The increased weight from cars and trucks was too much for the bridge to support so it collapsed.

The same analogy can be used to describe entrepreneurs. Sometimes we can get used to carrying so much weight we don't realize we are in danger of collapsing. We weren't built to sustain huge amounts of weight for prolonged periods of time. When I get stressed, my wife likes to suggest a vacation. But I've learned that vacations are not what help me (in fact, I usually come back with more on my mind and more to do). What I need to alleviate stress is help. For me, being stressed is not just about burnout and depletion of energy levels. My source of stress is the increased weight added by new roles and responsibilities as well as unexpected conflicts and complications. My stress comes from lacking the structural support for the weight I'm carrying.

So, with this realization, I began adding more organizational strength to my ventures. I shifted some of the weight and allowed others to carry some of it. Hiring the right person to whom I can delegate the source of my stress is better than any vacation. If you're going to be in this entrepreneurial business for the long haul, you too will need to learn how to manage stress. You were not built to carry too much weight.

How do you handle stress?

In the same way, faith by itself, if it is not accompanied by action, is dead.

(James 2:17, NIV)

Many would-be entrepreneurs have requested my advice and counsel. These people sit down with me and lay out their thoughtful and thorough business plans complete with solid, up-to-date sales data and market research. They have great answers for each of my questions, often giving specifics about their idea and their competition. They demonstrate that they have been very deliberate in thinking of their name, a logo and sometimes even branding materials. They have budgets, websites, domain names, and more.

Then they turn to me and ask: "Do you think I'm ready to launch?"

I tell them: "I can't answer that question, only you can. But if you're waiting on skywriting or some other sign to assure you that your business won't fail, falter, or flounder, then I'm afraid you will never get started. Risk is always part of the joy of being an entrepreneur—so embrace it!"

I know many of you have the same question. You've probably planned and prepared and studied and done all of the groundwork to launch your business. Yet, you are still waiting for a miraculous sign that now is the time. I tell you the same thing I tell those I meet with. Risk will always be a part of launching a venture—and even keeping it going. You have to sometimes follow Nike and "just do it."

Don't waste time in the present when you can be investing in your future. Do the hard work required to start your business, check the conditions and wind patterns, ask God to bless your efforts and give you guidance and wisdom—and then go!

What are you waiting on?

And afterward, I will pour out my Spirit on all people. Your sons and daughters
will prophesy, your old men will dream dreams, your young men will see visions.

(Joel 2:28, NIV)

I've entered my seventh decade of life. As I celebrated my birthday, I used the time to reflect on my past and take inventory of all I've been privileged to accomplish on this earth. I'm thankful for all God has instilled in me and for the faith to follow the path He set before me. However, I don't see sixty as a time to sit around and rest on my laurels. I have always looked to the future and anticipated the endless possibilities and potential that awaits. I believe the best is yet to come—for me and for you.

If you're going to live life to its fullest, I think you need to adopt this attitude, too. No matter where you are in life, you are uniquely equipped to bring your entrepreneurial vision to live. You have what it takes to grow your business into a thriving success and to leave a legacy of wisdom, wealth and worth to those behind you. In order to succeed, however, you must be willing to let go of excuses and find the courage to soar. Make up your mind that you're going to make decisions that will change the rest of your life. I know people who have wanted to become entrepreneurs all of their lives, but they never took the leap. They always considered the risk as too high. Instead, they stayed on the sidelines, read the books, and dreamed.

If this is you, I implore you to take action. Use what you've learned in this book to provide you with practical advice on getting started and sustaining a profitable business. I know you'd hate to finish this course in life without having pursued your dream. Whatever you do, take some action today. Start to make active plans to follow your dream and birth what is brewing inside of you. There's a cloud of witnesses who have gone on before you. They have broken barriers, stepped out on faith, and done what others may have considered impossible. And you can do the same—in your own unique way, with your own unique stamp.

It's time to soar!

What will you do today to actively pursue your dream?

> But don't just listen to God's word. You must do what it says. Otherwise, you are
> only fooling yourselves.   (James 1:22, NLT)

Now that you've read these daily readings and hopefully the book *Soar!*, you are better equipped to launch that business or move your existing business to another level. I pray you've received valuable information on taking steps toward a successful business. While absorbing information is critical, I want you to use the information. Take action. Take steps. Do more to make your dream a reality.

Make a list of steps you need to take. Focus on one at a time. Give yourself a realistic timeline to complete each step. Ask for help; get an accountability partner who can check up on you and make sure you have not stalled. The only direction you need to go is *forward* so you can soar.

The fact that you have read this book tells me that you have a dream inside of you. Let this book ignite the fire within—and use your action steps to keep that flame aburning. Someone somewhere wants what you have to offer. Don't deny them the chance of experiencing your God-given set of gifts and skills.

Don't allow your excuses to keep you trapped in complacency and inactivity. You still have life—make it count by sharing your gifts with others. You will be blessed from your activity—and all you offer will bless others. It's a win-win.

What steps will you take this week?

About the Author

T.D. Jakes is a #1 *New York Times* bestselling author of more than forty books and is the CEO of TDJ enterprises, LLP. He is the founder of the thirty-thousand-member Potter's House Church, and his television ministry program, *The Potter's Touch,* is watched by 3.3 million viewers every week. He has produced Grammy Award-winning music and such films as *Heaven Is For Real, Sparkle,* and *Jumping the Broom.* A master communicator, he hosts MegaFest, Woman Thou Art Loosed, and other conferences attended by tens of thousands. T. D. Jakes lives in Dallas with his wife and five children. Visit www.tdjakes.com.